Measuring Government Activity

OECD

ORGANISATION FOR ECONOMIC CO-OPERATION AND DEVELOPMENT

The OECD is a unique forum where the governments of 30 democracies work together to address the economic, social and environmental challenges of globalisation. The OECD is also at the forefront of efforts to understand and to help governments respond to new developments and concerns, such as corporate governance, the information economy and the challenges of an ageing population. The Organisation provides a setting where governments can compare policy experiences, seek answers to common problems, identify good practice and work to co-ordinate domestic and international policies.

The OECD member countries are: Australia, Austria, Belgium, Canada, the Czech Republic, Denmark, Finland, France, Germany, Greece, Hungary, Iceland, Ireland, Italy, Japan, Korea, Luxembourg, Mexico, the Netherlands, New Zealand, Norway, Poland, Portugal, the Slovak Republic, Spain, Sweden, Switzerland, Turkey, the United Kingdom and the United States. The Commission of the European Communities takes part in the work of the OECD.

OECD Publishing disseminates widely the results of the Organisation's statistics gathering and research on economic, social and environmental issues, as well as the conventions, guidelines and standards agreed by its members.

This work is published on the responsibility of the Secretary-General of the OECD. The opinions expressed and arguments employed herein do not necessarily reflect the official views of the Organisation or of the governments of its member countries.

Also available in French under the title:
Mesurer l'activité des administrations

Foreword

As public sector reforms continue across the OECD, there is a growing need for improved, evidence-based data on government activities and structures to enable country level changes to be seen in comparison with those undertaken elsewhere, and to provide a direction for the future. The OECD can build on its expertise in mapping and analyzing public management practices, processes and institutions by developing indicators that can be used by policy makers to benchmark government performance and link public management practices to performance outcomes.

This publication sets out the elements of a new approach to collecting data on public management. It introduces a comprehensive data classification and analysis framework and discusses in detail the challenges of output and outcome measurement in the public sector. It builds on three papers that were originally published in 2006 and reviewed technical alternatives for OECD data collection in public management.

This work was led by Nick Manning of the OECD Secretariat with major contributions from colleagues Dirk-Jan Kraan, Jana Malinska, Janos Bertok, Jon Hall and Erica Matthews; and Wouter Van Dooren, Miekatrien Streck and Geert Bouckaert of the University of Leuven. The development of the methodology was overseen by three informal editorial groups comprising leading government and academic experts drawn from across the OECD, and in close collaboration with other OECD Directorates, particularly the Economics Department and the Statistics Directorate. The book was edited by Christopher Pollitt, Geert Bouckaert and Wouter van Dooren. Jennifer Allain, Jordan Holt and Zsuzsanna Lonti prepared the book for publication.

Table of Contents

Chapter 1. Introduction...**7**
1.1. Some key distinctions...9
1.2. Measures for different audiences and purposes.....................................13

Chapter 2. Why Measure Government Activities? **15**
2.1. Measurement matters 15
2.2. How can international comparable data assist governments? 17
2.2. The risks of measurement...24
2.3. The risks of non-use and of absent or weak data...................................36

Chapter 3. Output Measurement: Key Issues **43**
3.1. Technical issues..44
3.2. Utilisation...46
3.3. Adding it up..60

Chapter 4. Outcome Measurement: Key Issues **63**
4.1. Introduction 63
4.2. What outcome measures do governments use?......................................64
4.3. Origins and growth of well-being measures...67
4.4. Measures can provide a frame or vision for subsequent policy decisions.........69
4.5. Filling an apparent gap...73
4.6. Developing comparative measures concerning trust in government...............78
4.7. Developing comparative measures concerning equity and economic and fiscal stability 83

Chapter 5. Improving the Measurement of Government Activities...................**87**
5.1. The scope of data collection...87
5.2. Establishing a coherent data classification framework..........................90
5.3. OECD's role..95

Annex A. Co-ordinating with Data Collection Developments in Non-OECD Countries...**101**

Annex B. Outcome Measures of Well-being Included in at Least Two National Publications Tracking Government Performance...........................**107**

Glossary...**111**

Bibliography **115**

Tables

Table 2.1 The major types of performance indicator 16
Table 2.2 Reform trajectories 23
Table 3.1 Functional classification versus measurability 46
Table 3.2 Use of output indicators (excluding contracts subject to
       judicial enforcement) 48
Table 3.3 Use of output measures 53
Table 3.4 The uses of output measures and their contribution
       to decision-making 54
Table 3.5 Relationship between the basis of output measures and their use 57
Table 3.6 New Zealand output classes 58
Table 3.7 Tradeoffs between the basis and use of output measures 60
Table 5.1 Key sites of public management activity 89
Table 5.2 Currently available data 95

Figures

Figure 2.1 Disaggregated public sector production process 17
Figure 2.2 A suggested data structure of internationally comparable
       data on public management 18
Figure 2.3 The CAF Model 20
Figure 2.4 Manipulation of measures and of outputs 26
Figure 3.1 Ease of output measurement 45
Figure 5.1 The basic public sector production process 90

Boxes

Box 2.1 The Common Assessment Framework (CAF) and benchmarking .. 20
Box 2.2 Summary of OECD criteria for constructing composite indicators 34
Box 2.3 Some dimensions of public sector reform 35
Box 3.1 Providing output information to Parliament in Australia
       and the United Kingdom 51
Box 4.1 An increasing focus on capital within well-being indicators 65
Box 4.2 Apparent criteria for well-being indicators 66
Box 4.3 Outcomes as a broad focus for policy thinking 70
Box 4.4 Enthusiasts note that outcome measurement offers performance
       dividends 72
Box 4.5 Governance indicators 74
Box 4.6 Development goals for state services in New Zealand 76
Box 4.7 Selecting executive governance outcomes 77
Box 5.1 Compliance with the OECD Quality Framework for Statistical
       Activities 97
Box 1A.1 OECD collaboration on public sector reform with middle
       and high income (non-OECD) countries 102

Chapter 1. Introduction

Nowadays it is hard to imagine a sustained debate on government performance that would not include some reference to the money spent (inputs), the quality of government processes, the quality and quantity of government outputs, and the outcomes (or lack of them) eventually achieved. Very extensive academic and practitioner literature are devoted to the subject of these aspects of government performance, literature which stretches back for at least a quarter of a century.

Yet the measurements of these dimensions (inputs, processes, outputs, outcomes) are frequently frail, crude or simply missing. This is true even at national level, but far more so for the purpose of international comparisons. Some existing comparisons are based on surprisingly weak and narrow data. Indeed, many expert commentators agree that existing comparative data on government activity are shot through with problems and weaknesses. Just a few specific areas stand out as beacons of what could, in principle, be achieved (especially some in education and healthcare, such as the OECD Programme for International Student Assessment (PISA) studies or certain comparisons of the effectiveness of particular medical procedures).

The challenges facing comparative measurement go far beyond the issue of unreliable or missing measures. Before a single measure has been made there are significant difficulties to be tackled in the very conceptualisation or categorisation of the "units" under discussion. Frequently used terms such as "government", "civil service" or "public sector" turn out to have different meanings and different domains in different countries.

These widely acknowledged data constraints have been one important factor prompting the OECD's current Government at a Glance initiative. This programme is aimed at improving the general quality and comparability of government activity data and, more specifically, at producing a new regular publication, *Government at a Glance*, the first issue of which is planned for late in 2009. Such a publication should enable more securely based benchmarking between countries, and should encourage more effective OECD-wide lesson learning with respect to sector efficiency, process/output relationships, issues of capacity change and a variety of other aspects.

One feature of this initiative will be an attempt to stabilise an agreed set of categories for institutional domains (what do we mean by "government", "the public sector", etc.); for stages in the process of producing public goods and service; and for specific aspects of those stages (particularly "outputs" and "outcomes"). This may sound rather dull and technical, but it is not possible to have an effective international dialogue without a standardised vocabulary.

It could be argued that this is a particularly propitious time for such an exercise. For the last quarter of a century many governments have been reconsidering and adjusting their roles. Some governments have chosen widespread privatisation of public utilities. An overlapping, but also partly distinct, group of countries have significantly increased the role of the private sector inside the public sector, through a variety of means including public-private partnerships, franchising and contracting out. Elsewhere ideas of "co-production" have seen significant involvement of citizen groups and civil society associations in public service planning, delivery and evaluation. In many places, while the government may have retreated from directly providing services itself, it has increased its role as a regulator. In all these cases the boundary between the public sector and the private sector has shifted and taken on new and sometimes ambiguous meanings. A reconsideration of what government does, and how we classify and measure this activity is therefore overdue.

The present volume comprises an edited synthesis of technical papers originally produced for the OECD Public Governance Committee in the autumn of 2006. Broadly, the four main chapters deal with the following issues:

- Chapter 2 offers an overview of the reasons why government activity should be measured and the main approaches to the task of measurement. It also acknowledges that there are risks associated with measurement – risks which can be minimised but not always entirely eliminated.

- Chapter 3 focuses on issues concerning non-financial output measures, including not only their technical characteristics but also the different behaviours the act of producing such measures may induce. The existence of output measures may lead staff to strive for improved performance, but they may also lead to the neglect of non-measured dimensions or to "gaming" in which either the output itself is adjusted or the measurements are distorted in order to achieve the appearance (rather than the reality) of a "good" performance.[1]

- Chapter 4 examines the challenging issue of outcome measurement. It argues that it would be both feasible and very valuable to begin to develop a set of measures specifically concerned with the outcomes of "executive governance". These would address outcomes in the areas of public confidence in government, equity in government actions and stability in fiscal and economic outcomes.

- Finally, Chapter 5 sets out a possible way forward for data collection concerning public management in the OECD. This illustrates the amount and direction of work that is necessary if more accurate and meaningful international comparisons of government activity are to be achieved.

This book is presented not at all as the "final word" on these technical issues, but rather as an opening contribution towards addressing fundamental problems of measurement that have hampered international analysis and debate for many years.

1.1. Some key distinctions

The measurement of government activity is both complex and hotly debated. As a recent expert text put it: "The performance of public organisations cannot be reduced to a single dimension, and is inescapably contestable" (Boyne *et al.*, 2006). To assist the reader, it may be useful briefly to identify certain key distinctions which run throughout the more detailed technical discussions in the following pages.

- the output/outcome distinction;
- the individual/collective distinction;
- transactional perspectives versus production/provision perspectives ;
- the distinction between "objective" and "subjective" measures;
- tight and loose linkages between measures and other decisions.

1.1.1. The output/outcome distinction

Traditionally, governments have tended to focus on how much they spend on different activities or programmes – on the financial inputs to government activity. More recently a good deal of the management literature has concentrated on processes – how matters are organised and what techniques or organisational structures are used to transform the inputs into goods and services. Both inputs and processes remain important foci for interest, analysis and debate. However, during the past two decades many countries have striven to obtain a clearer picture of what they get for all these inputs and processes – in other words what are the outputs and outcomes?

The need to distinguish between outputs and outcomes is accepted by most (not all) public management experts, even if the borderline between the two is sometimes hard to draw. As is discussed in the remainder of this book, definitions vary, but in principle the difference is one between the immediate results of government activity (grants made, children taught, driving licenses issued) and the final impacts of these activities (what is produced by those spending the grants, what the children have learned, whether the roads are safer and more orderly because of the licensing of drivers). The former (immediate results) are the outputs, the latter (eventual impacts on society) are the outcomes. One very significant difference between the two is that whereas it is usually reasonable to hold government responsible for outputs it is often not reasonable to hold them entirely responsible for outcomes, because many other factors beyond government's control may intervene to influence the final impacts on society. For example, a grant to a firm can be made quickly and correctly but some sudden change in global economic conditions may undermine the commercial viability of the project receiving the support so that it does not actually achieve its intended outcomes. In practice the line from first outputs to last outcomes may be a long and complicated one, with various intermediate actions and reactions.

The position taken here will be that it is vital to attempt to secure good measures of both outputs and outcomes, but that the measurement problems and the conclusions that may legitimately be drawn from such measures are likely to be somewhat different for the two categories.

1.1.2. The individual/collective distinction

Some government services are consumed mainly by identifiable individuals (education, social security benefits) while others are mainly consumed collectively (defence, air pollution control). Some are usually consumed collectively but could in principle be consumed individually (*e.g.* public roads, where charging systems are then introduced).

This distinction is particularly important for those who wish to take an economic perspective on government (less so for other approaches). Individually consumed services can be measured as individual transactions (see next section) which opens up the possibility of using a range of standard techniques of economic analysis, originally developed for use in market environments where individual producers face individual consumers. These techniques work much less well where individual consumers cannot be identified.

1.1.3. Transactional perspectives versus production/provision perspectives

As indicated in the previous section, economic approaches frequently rely on a conceptualisation of activity (including government activity) as a series of transactions between "buyers" and "sellers". By contrast, public administration and public management experts often conceptualise government activity as a complex production process in which various skills and resources are combined in different ways to produce goods and services and regulatory decisions. Rather than using the metaphor of the producer/consumer, the nature and level of provision is seen as being defined through the politico-administrative system. In democratic societies, the ultimate accountability is in the hands of the citizens. Different concepts inform these two perspectives and, to some extent, each uses its own techniques to construct a picture of what is going on and how it should be measured/assessed. This distinction interacts with, but is conceptually different from the individual/collective distinction (above). The production/provision perspective reminds us of the necessarily political nature of government activity, of its democratic foundations and consequent multiple accountabilities.

In the text that follows no attempt is made to pronounce one or other of these perspectives as "better". Each gives a distinctive and potentially valuable view of government activity. Adherents of the two perspectives may arrive at different answers about such important issues as public sector productivity and quality. For one, the quest may be to perfect the measurement of GDP per capita, while for the other such a traditional economic measure is inherently unsatisfactory for many purposes because of what it leaves out.

1.1.4. Objective and subjective measures

Some analysts like to draw a distinction between "objective" and "subjective" measures. For example, government consumption as a percentage of GDP might be classified as an objective measure, whereas measures of citizen trust in government or citizen fear of crime would be said to be "subjective" because they rest on the expression of individual opinions. Many or most of the "well-being" measures that have become popular in the past decade or so (and which are discussed in Chapter 4) would, from this point of view, be seen as "subjective".

However, an increasing number of experts reject the objective/subjective distinction as too simple. After all, the definitions of both "government consumption" and "GDP" are socially constructed by particular authorities at particular times (and are also changed from time to time). In some countries the official definition of an unemployed person has changed 10 or more times in the last 20 years, so it is hard to claim that this is completely "objective". As one group of quite "tough", quantitatively-oriented social scientists put it recently: "All measures are ultimately 'perceptual' rather than 'factual'" (Andrews *et al.*, 2006), although there remains a significant difference between measures of opinions and measures of events.

We will not, therefore, draw an artificial and highly contestable line between "objective" measures and "others". The following sections certainly engage with indicators of "well-being" as well as more traditional economic and financial measures. However, for all measures we need to ask how valid and reliable and stable they are, and to what extent they are independently assessed to be so.

1.1.5. Tight/loose linkages between measures and decisions

Technical characteristics such as validity and reliability are tremendously important, but ultimately an assessment of the measurement potential has to go much wider than that. It has to consider how measures are actually used, by whom and for what purposes. In this regard one commonly used distinction is between having a "tight" or a "loose" link between the measure and consequent decisions. In sport, for example, we are used to tight linkages: once a squash player has scored nine points he or she wins the game. Similarly, in some public sector contexts, linkages can be automatic: under the UK Research Assessment Exercise, university departments rated at five stars automatically received more research money than those rated only three or four.

More commonly, perhaps, the linkage is looser than this. The "score" on a particular measure becomes an input to a subsequent discussion, and decisions are only taken after that discussion. The performance measure then becomes one piece of information among others which inform decisions, rather than the factor that determines the decision. As Chapter 2 makes clear, there are arguments for and against both tight and loose linkages, but the choice is a fundamental one. One influence on such choices is, of course, the quality of the measurements themselves. Basing decisions on tight, automatic formulae may be very dangerous unless the measures are valid, reliable, comprehensive and not too vulnerable to "gaming".[2] Where such exemplary measures are not available, it may be better to treat measures as "tin-openers", opening up a discussion, than as "dials" which definitively represent the achievements of public organisations (Carter *et al.*, 1992). Whilst these issues are explicitly discussed in some sections of what follows it may be valuable to bear in mind considerations of the most appropriate use of measures throughout your reading.

1.2. Measures for different audiences and purposes

To take the issue of the use of measures one step further, it should be noted that, even within government, different audiences may need different kinds of measures to serve different kinds of purpose. One may draw a parallel here with the evolution of budgetary systems, where the progressive addition of functions to traditional budgets (input control, then macro-economic management, then efficient resource allocation, then improving programme management) has brought advantages but also considerable new challenges. Thus, to take a fairly simple threefold approach, measures may be used to assist in decisions concerning:

- macro-economic management;
- the allocation of resources between sectors or programmes;
- the improvement of the operational management of specific programmes or projects or services.

Each of these purposes is likely to concern a somewhat different audience which will want rather different types of measure. In every case it may well be possible to learn from international comparisons, but in every case these lessons will need to be translated into local contexts. "Modernisation is dependent on contexts. While all governments are being affected by global trends, there are no public management cure-alls" (OECD, 2005c). Similarly, the establishment of a set of common measures of government activity does not at all presuppose some kind of automatic application to decision-making.

Notes

1. Gaming has been usefully defined as "reactive subversion such as 'hitting the target and missing the point' or reducing performance where targets do not apply" (Bevan and Hood, 2005). It is discussed in more detail in Chapters 3 and 4 of this publication.

2. See section 2.2.2.

Chapter 2. Why Measure Government Activities?

2.1. Measurement matters

This section will consider, in turn, the direct advantages of measuring government activity, the risks which can attend such measurement, and, finally, the risks which arise through not attempting to measure.

How government activities are measured, matters. Given the size of government and its role in the economy, the contribution of government to national economic growth is of great significance, especially when looking at change rates over time. Recent work in the United Kingdom highlights that changing the basis of measurement of government activity can increase or decrease the measure of GDP significantly (Atkinson *et al.*, 2005). Beyond economics, measuring government activity is important because of the size of its activities and the consequent need to understand what it is achieving with the very significant expenditures (across the OECD, between 30% and 54% of GDP in 2006). Considerable "measurement communities" have grown up around the ideas of public service quality, benchmarking and user satisfaction. The public sector's achievements, or otherwise, emerge in the quality and nature of the goods and services it provides, its redistributive activities, and in the nature of its regulation of market and individual behaviour.

As many have noted, the notion of performance is seen as fundamental to the modern state (Matheson *et al.*, 2006; Schick, 2005). This has led to significant reforms within government – and to a deluge of managerial and political rhetoric about the measurement of performance (Boyne *et al.*, 2006; Pollitt and Bouckaert, 2004). These developments are based around the notion that, as the state is responsible for such a large and changing array of services and regulatory tasks, it must quantify its promises and measure its actions in ways that allow citizens, managers and politicians to make meaningful decisions about increasingly complex state activities. However, "performance" in this context has been used in so many ways that it becomes difficult to draw broader conclusions for action about how to measure it and what to do with the results. This problem arises for two main reasons. First, the term "performance" seems increasingly to be a rhetorical device to imply that a managerial approach is new or more focused – implying a break with the past and with previous managerial models that were not as "cutting edge". Second, performance measures can capture aspects of input, process, output and outcome, and any number of derived ratios between these.[1] Table 2.1 sets out a range of such measures, excluding measures of agency business processes. It suggests that performance measures can, and should, include many aspects that are idiosyncratic and specific to the time, programme, agency and existing public sector culture rendering them unsuitable for any broader comparative work. Any of these can be used as the basis for a performance measure. Where outputs are hard to measure, outcomes are more likely to be used albeit with considerable caution because of the attribution problems.

Table 2.1. The major types of performance indicator[1]

Single indicators		
Indicators on input	What goes into the system? Which resources are used?	
Indicators on output	Which products and services are delivered? What is the quality of these products and services?	
Indicators on intermediate outcomes	What are the direct consequences of the output?	
Indicators on final outcomes	What are the outcomes achieved that are significantly attributable to the output?	
Indicators on the environment	What are the contextual factors that influence the output?	
Ratio indicators		
Efficiency	Costs/output[2]	These measures are valid only to the extent that there is a clear causal relationship[3]
Productivity	Output/input	
Effectiveness	Output/outcome (intermediate or final)	
Cost-effectiveness	Cost/outcome (intermediate or final)	

1. These indicators omit measures of agency business processes. As the Canadian Treasury Board Management Accountability Framework demonstrates, various metrics can be also be developed of: *i)* effectiveness of mechanisms to promulgate public service values; *ii)* strength of internal governance and leadership; *iii)* effectiveness of arrangements for staff learning, fostering innovation and change management; *iv)* clarity of the policy framework and policy capacity; *v)* risk management; *vi)* human resource management; *vii)* stewardship (including capital assets and it infrastructure); and *viii)* compliance with mandatory authorities and delegations. See *www.tbs-sct.gc.ca/maf-crg/.*

2. In econometric analysis, efficiency is seen as the distance of an observation's input and output vector from the production frontier. Here, we use the definition that is more common in public administration, *i.e.* the ratio of costs to output.

3. Suppose a health service spends money on procedures which evidence based medicine suggests are useless or worse than useless – for example most tonsillectomies. Health statuses may well be rising, for completely independent reasons. However, we would not want to conclude that expenditures on these procedures were cost effective: quite the reverse.

Source: Developed from Sterck *et al.* (2006).

Within this classification, output measures have two distinct advantages over the more generic notion of performance indicators – at least in providing opportunities for lesson-learning. First, there has been extensive experience and conceptual analysis of output measures in the context of the System of National Accounts (SNA). Although SNA discussions emphasise the economic conception of outputs (an issue which is discussed further below), they provide an analysis of the implications of aggregation and of options for maintaining data quality that is unmatched in any other measure of public sector activity.[2] Second, as Table 2.1 makes clear, output measures are implicated in all measures of economy, efficiency, productivity and effectiveness. They are, in effect, the building blocks of most performance indicators.

2.2. How can international comparable data assist governments?

Figure 2.1 shows a somewhat standard approach to classifying the stages in the public sector production process. In this subsection we will set out some of the general ways in which, using this classification, good international comparative data can be used to assist governments.

Figure 2.1. Disaggregated public sector production process

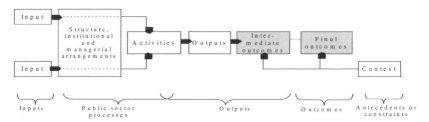

Source: Based on Van Dooren *et al.* (2006), Hatry (1999), Boyne and Law (2004), Pollitt and Bouckaert (2004), and Algemene Rekenkamer (2006).

As Figure 2.2 shows, the basic structure of international comparative data is that of a cube – with the three key dimensions of countries, years and data classifications.

Figure 2.2. A suggested data structure of internationally comparable data on public management

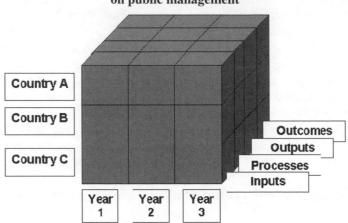

Drawing on different comparisons within this cube, internationally comparable public management data can help governments and other analysts in two main ways:

1. For individual countries, it can enable robust benchmarking between countries, using common units of analysis, facilitating a structured practitioner dialogue and moving away from simplistic best practice, uncritically promoting new developments.

2. It can contribute to OECD-wide lesson-learning concerning:

    *   Sector efficiency and broader measures of institutional effectiveness, providing insights into the results of providing services via different institutional and managerial arrangements.

    *   Observed relationships (which changes in public sector processes are associated with which changes in outputs?)

    *   Absorptive capacity (can public sector production be scaled up quickly following significant increases in sector expenditures, and the converse?)

2.2.1. For individual countries

Benchmarking and structured practitioner dialogue

Managing within the public sector is, and likely will remain, an art as much as a science, and practitioner experiences will continue to be a core source of guidance concerning future developments. Those practitioner experiences are best shared within a structured dialogue however, and there has been some concern about reform excesses that have resulted from inappropriately enthusiastic borrowing of others' experiences. Improved availability of internationally comparable data can assist in framing that dialogue through benchmarking – a structured debate between practitioners, agencies or governments concerning how and why things are different between them.

Proponents often link benchmarking with an assumption that if "best practices" have been developed in one setting, then it offers a vehicle for identifying how key elements might be exported and usefully adapted.[3] Whether or not one subscribes to the concept that there are best practices independent of time and place, making comparisons within carefully selected parameters can sustain a productive debate about how and why things differ between settings and options for reform (Cowper and Samuels, 1997).

The key assumption of benchmarking is that the comparisons are not, per se, evaluative. Benchmarking is done to open up the reasons why performances are different – to induce a thorough discussion of underlying processes and contexts. The purpose of benchmarking is thus to open up issues for subsequent investigation – to provoke interest in deeper examinations.[4] The OECD public sector peer review exercises (Budget Reviews, Human Resource Management Reviews, Regulatory Reviews, E-government Reviews, etc.) are ultimately based on benchmarking, and as data become more available, these reviews will be strengthened with a broader array of comparative data around which to initiate discussions.

Benchmarking approaches to common challenges

Benchmarking can be used to compare inputs, processes, outputs or outcomes. Much of the practitioner literature emphasises its use to compare intermediate outcomes – very particularly customer satisfaction and perceived service quality.[5]

The key is to define a series of variables, and then whether through self-assessment as with the Common Assessment Framework (CAF – see Box 2.1) or through objective measures, to compare the results as a component of a structured dialogue concerning their significance and their likely impact on agency performance.

The European Institute of Public Administration CAF allows an organisation to fill in the evaluation form on-line after the self-assessment has been conducted. The achieved results will remain anonymous, but the organisation will get feedback on its scoring against the average of other organisations that have used the CAF in the same country or the same sector of activity. The self-assessment results will be part of the European CAF database, which contains information with regard to the organisations that have used the CAF, their sector of activity, the size of the organisations in terms of personnel and contact persons. By offering key information the database can help public sector organisations identify suitable benchmarking partners.

**Box 2.1 The Common Assessment Framework (CAF)
and benchmarking**

The Common Assessment Framework (CAF) is a result of the co-operation between the European Union Ministers responsible for Public Administration. A new version of the framework was prepared in 2002 by the Innovative Public Services Group, an informal working group of national experts set up by the European Union Directors General in order to promote exchanges and co-operation in modernising government and public service delivery in EU member states.

The CAF is both a free-standing self-assessment tool, and a structured method for sharing information between agencies about nine functional areas.

Figure 2.3 The CAF Model

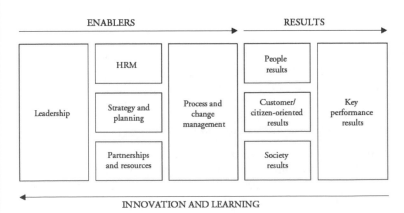

Source : European Institution of Public Administration, *The Common Assessment Framework (CAF): Improving an Organisation through Self-Assessment*, (2002).

2.2.2. OECD-wide lesson-learning

Developing measures for public spending efficiency

Developments in measuring public spending efficiency look promising. Non-parametrical approaches have been increasingly used based on Data Envelopment Analysis (DEA). Comparative country data can further enrich these analyses. The basic idea of this approach is to view schools (for example) as productive units which use inputs (*e.g.* teaching time or public spending on education) and produce education services (outputs) whose quality characteristics can be measured through the proficiency level of pupils (*e.g.* tests from the OECD Programme for International Student Assessment). The method produces measures of relative efficiency by deriving an "efficiency frontier", *i.e.* the production frontier which envelops the set of observations on inputs consumed and outputs produced by individual units or countries. The distance of observations from the frontier is then measured to obtain efficiency scores. Once the "efficient frontier" has been defined, the relative efficiency of public service providers can be measured as the distance of observations to the frontier, either in an international or national context (sub-national governments or groups of providers).

This approach allows benchmarking and the detection of sources of inefficiency (*e.g.* the mix or volume of inputs used and/or their costs). An attractive feature is that it does not require an a priori judgment on the desirable output/outcome level for each public spending programme which may reflect differences in societal tastes and choices. Rather, it allows an assessment of whether inputs are efficiently used to deliver given outputs.

One key concern is whether the output measure captures the value of the service. For example, in considering the use of PISA scores as the quality characteristic of an output, there is a risk that the PISA tests do not indicate the effectiveness of education – whether a 15-year old with a high PISA score is on the way to a successful career in something useful is not clear. The consequence could be that some amount of the resources which the analysis registers as "inefficiency" is in fact used to teach the students something useful which is not captured by PISA scores.

Stochastic frontier analysis is a parametric method which starts from the estimation of a production function and then distinguishes the distance from separate observations into estimation error (noise) on the one hand and inefficiency on the other.

Typically DEA analysis and stochastic frontier analysis use a very limited number of output variables which might not fully capture the value of the services.

Another concern is the way in which the institutional drivers of efficiency are conceived. These can conceal prior assumptions concerning preferred institutional arrangements within the public sector (implying that decentralisation is always efficiency enhancing for example) particularly when composite indicators are constructed, and the construction of any measures of the institutional drivers of efficiency should be based on solid theoretical grounds.

Developing measures of institutional effectiveness

While efficiency or productivity builds on the relationship between inputs and outputs, institutional effectiveness examines the relationships between, on the one hand, public sector structures and processes and, on the other, some types of outcome. As will be discussed below, care must be taken to ensure that any outcomes are indeed directly attributable to government activities. Thus, for example, improved data could, over time, provide insights into the results of different oversight arrangements in relation to changed measures of public trust.

Trajectories

Pollitt and Bouckaert (2004) identify, tentatively, some reform trajectories, noting that these are not neat and tidy, or indeed predestined, but that they seem to represent paths which OECD member countries seemed to be attempting to follow in their modernisation efforts.

Table 2.2 Reform trajectories

	Budget reforms	Accounting reforms	Audit reforms
Direction of change	1. Input-oriented line item budget 2. + some performance information 3. + revised format and content 4. + revised procedures and timing 5. + revised method of charging (accrual basis)	1. Cash-based 2. Double-entry bookkeeping 3. Accrual accounting with extended cost calculation supported by performance measurement system	1. Traditional financial and compliance audit 2. + elements of performance and evaluation 3. Institutionalised financial, compliance and performance auditing

Source: Based on Pollitt and Bouckaert (2004).

Monitoring of public sector processes over time will allow for a more robust assessment of the degree to which such trajectories are found in practice and whether significant departure from the mainstream is associated with any distinctive differences in context or in outputs/outcomes.[6]

In the current public management climate, with a strong focus on "performance orientation" (Schick, 2005), one particularly interesting trajectory to track concerns changes in the way in which performance is measured – the nature of the output and outcome measures and how they are used. This would assist in reviewing the degree to which measures are "churned", either because they must be changed regularly as they inevitably lose their impact over time (Thiel and Leeuw, 2002), or because of a somewhat cynical attempt to maximise the apparent performance improvement (Talbot, 1996).

Contribution analysis

Mayne (1999) points out that one key value of monitoring change over time is to assist in unpacking complex attribution problems in examining public sector outputs and outcomes. Since agency or programme designs generally cannot be adjusted experimentally to assess impact, the challenge is how to determine whether, and in what proportion, programme activities and public sector processes contribute to outputs, and similarly which outputs contribute significantly to which outcomes. He notes that "where the programme activities have varied over time, showing that outcomes have varied in a consistent manner with the variation in activities can strengthen the argument that the activities have indeed made a difference. In the simplest example, if an expected outcome has been observed after (and not before) the program activity has started up, this suggests the program is having an effect. In a more complicated case, if the outcome improves at sites (or at times) where the program has been implemented but not at others (such as a national programme operating at many locations), the case for making a difference is even stronger" (Mayne, 1999).

Absorptive capacity

Large bureaucracies, public or private, can find challenges in ensuring that outputs increase appropriately with increases in inputs. When resources are scaled up rapidly, it is widely held that a significant part of those additional resources will be used to improve working conditions and incomes, or simply be wasted (Social and Cultural Planning Office, 2004). There are also more technical reasons why, at least in the short term, increased inputs might be associated with negative productivity growth rates. It is probable that the impact of information technology on productivity in the public sector mirrors that in the private sector, with the associated organisational changes reducing the short-term benefits from new technology due to disruption of production processes (Dawson *et al.*, 2005). The evidence seemingly suggests that in the United Kingdom, output growth lagged behind the increase in inputs used during the period 1995 to 2001, implying, on some measures, a fall in public sector productivity. However, other explanations for this development might include the need for spending on long-term investments and weak output measures (Pritchard, 2003).

Time series data will allow some analysis of the absorptive capacity of government organisations, allowing cross-country comparative analysis of the impact of softer budget constraints following significant increases in sector expenditures.

2.2. The risks of measurement

Whilst the arguments for measuring government activities are very strong, there are also risks. As the practice of measurement has grown – across many jurisdictions and sectors – awareness of these risks have also grown, to the point that now there is a substantial practitioner and academic literature concerned with them (*e.g.* Bevan and Hood, 2006; Radin, 2006).

In many cases the risks cannot be entirely eliminated – and it would be foolish to claim that they can. Rather, it is sometimes a case of pursuing more and better measurement in the full consciousness that certain kinds of risks arise, and that these must be managed so as to minimise them.

There are two primary risks associated with the use of measures within government. First, the literature suggests that scarce political, managerial and practitioner time can be diverted towards the production and consideration of measures which, although important, can only represent one contribution to decisions concerning planning or accountability and control. Second, there is the ever-present risk of gaming or unintended perverse outcomes being stimulated by the presence of measurement.

2.2.1. Demanding scarce political and managerial attention

The challenge in measures is one of balancing managerial and political time for both output and outcome measures. Because outcome measures provide an attractive topic for policy makers, not least because they are high level and visionary, they are particularly seductive – even at the risk of requiring a disproportionate amount of limited management time. Thus while outcome measures can usefully contribute to decisions concerning planning and concerning accountability and control (both in providing a basis for discussion about results achieved and about the quality of government outputs), and can equally usefully provide a frame or a vision for subsequent policy decisions, they do not remove the need for government to control spending and to select modes of production which enhance efficiency.

The Minister of Finance for the Netherlands noted this risk of being distracted from the basics in arguing for cautious sequencing in budget reforms: "I believe that things should be done in the proper sequence. I think that, for example, introducing accrual accounting for central government when accounting capacity still falls short and spending controls are weak is not the way to go forward … The same is true when budgets are primarily based on outputs and outcomes while fiscal rules are non-existent and the position of the Minister of Finance is relatively weak" (Zalm, 2004).

2.2.2. Gaming

Gaming refers to the strategic reaction of individuals, organisations or countries to the use of measures. Two kinds of reactions can be distinguished. One entails the manipulation of the measures that are selected. In this case, the operations remain the same but the representation of these operations by means of the indicators is deliberately skewed. This results in a loss of the quality the data. The alternative is manipulation of the output itself – "teaching the test" as it is sometimes called in education. This usually results in a loss of the quality of the output. A combination of both is also possible.

Figure 2.4 Manipulation of measures and of outputs

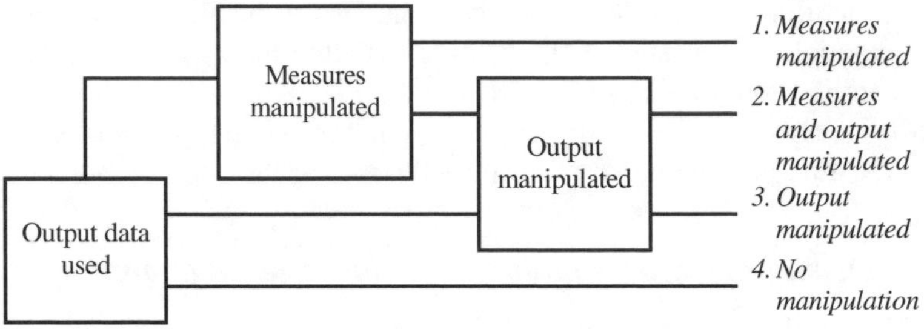

1. Measures manipulated
2. Measures and output manipulated
3. Output manipulated
4. No manipulation

Source: Developed from Van Dooren *et al.* (2006).

Gaming normally arises from principal/agent problems, where the service provider is left with a set of interests/incentives which differ from those of the service users. In principle, the solution is to align the producers' interests and incentives as closely as possible with those of users. This means that the target and incentive structure for providers needs to be designed accordingly.

Loss of quality in the output

Many empirical studies show that measurement can have a negative effect as it can lead to the neglect of unmeasured or unmeasurable dimensions of quality of service delivery. In the extreme case, many of these problems have historical parallels in the challenges that the former Soviet Union found in operating its central planning system. Thus Heinrich (1999), for example, observed that an emphasis on cost-per-placement measurements in a job-training program had a negative impact on service quality. This had earlier been described by Berliner (1956) in the context of the Soviet production targets. The use of monthly production quota led to "storming" at the end of the month. Repairs and maintenance were postponed to the next month that, in turn, led to a new rush at the end of the next month.

Bevan and Hood (2006) document three well-recognised gaming problems:[7]

- *Ratchet effects* refer to the consequences of central resource managers basing next year's targets on this year's performance. The effect of this is that managers have an incentive to reduce their output increases to a modest increment so that expectations and future targets will be set at a low level.[8]

- *Threshold effects* describe the tendency to focus agency attention on those outputs that are near to the required level of output. This leads to the concentration of effort on outputs that are just below the required level at the expense of others, ignoring the best (on the basis that these outputs will meet the test without effort) and the worst (on the basis that the reward is outweighed by the cost of improving these to the minimum standard).

- *Distortion* refers to the achievement of output improvements in areas that are measured at the expense of unmeasured aspects of performance.[9]

Although the theoretical concerns have been well known for some time, the evidence of gaming in practice has seemingly come as something of a surprise to policy makers. There has been extensive debate in the United Kingdom on the politically sensitive revelation that hospital waiting-time targets led to cancellations, and consequently longer waiting times before appointments could be made. The Public Administration Select Committee (2003) concluded that in such cases, perversely, measurement was leading to less rather than more output.[10]

Loss of quality in the data

Manipulation can take place further upstream. Manipulation of measurement, intentionally or otherwise, comes in many guises. The measures can simply be artificially inflated or deflated (Bouckaert and Balk, 1991; Smith, 1995). Less perniciously, measurement can suggest false trend data as more and more of the outputs are being uncovered than were previously assumed to exist (Bouckaert and Balk, 1991). An example is the number of violations of human rights reported by Amnesty International. This may be because of a real worsening of the situation – but could also be caused by the establishment of a higher number of observations. Measurement systems may get "polluted" (Bouckaert, 1995) as the concepts and definitions are interpreted differently. The confusion in the term "performance" places this concept at particularly high risk for this problem.

Finally, performance information may be manipulated by aggregating or disaggregating data (Perrin, 1998; Winston, 1993). Lesser performance may be obscured by more, or less, aggregate indicators. Separate indicators can be combined in composite indicators which have the benefit of simplicity. Decision-makers with limited time or the public with limited insight into complex policy matters are helped with a universal assessment of performance. Yet, by choosing and weighing the measures, organisations may hide problematic aspects of their performance. It may also happen the other way round. An organisation may look for more detail until the performance is satisfactory.

There is not yet an established practice in governments for auditing the quality of non-financial information, despite the longstanding tradition of auditing financial information. This is discussed in more detail below.

2.2.3. Mitigating gaming problems

The need to mitigate gaming is not, ex ante, an argument against the development and use of indicators – but experience is increasingly showing the degree to which gaming opportunities must be consciously limited through technical improvements in measurement (including "triangulation" – the collection of data from several independent sources) and through care in their use (grouping performance information measures so that perverse responses can be monitored, and gaining the trust and involvement of those being measured in the system, so that they will themselves work for its integrity).[11]

However, and perhaps more fundamentally, in addition to these technical approaches that can bolster the quality of measures which are subject to gaming, the way in which indicators are used must be considered. Proponents of the more modest use of output data argue that each refinement of an indicator will lead to correspondingly refined forms of gaming. They suggest that indicators will never catch the "real thing" however refined and however subtle the measuring methods. Clearly gaming will prove less worthwhile to the extent that output data hold a more moderate place in programme assessment alongside other forms of information (client satisfaction, qualitative evaluation, cost-benefit analysis). We return to this issue of the tightness of the "coupling" later in this book.

Technical approaches to the quality of output data

The loss of quality of outputs through the ratchet or threshold effects, or through distortions in agency behaviour can be somewhat addressed in the design of a measurement system. One way to achieve this is to create indicators that measure aspects of quality of output in addition to the quantities: timeliness, processing time and accuracy of output delivery are frequently measured quality aspects. Indicators can also be designed that provide incentives to institute in-depth quality reviews of a sample of outputs (*e.g.* measuring the number of performance audits that are reviewed against auditing standards). Other indicators can draw attention to the quality aspects of the outliers – guarding more directly against the threshold effect.

Indicators can also be derived that assess the quality of the outputs by looking at the intermediate outcomes. While there are difficulties in measuring quality by means of the satisfaction of the client groups, output quality indicators can also include the quality of internal service delivery.

Whatever the details of the strategy, the result is two sets of indicators, one emphasising physical volume and cost, and one emphasising the quality of output (assessed either by looking at the quality of the output or at the outcome). These sets of indicators are not easily combined. A linkage between the output cost/volume indicators and the quality of output indicators can be made through weighted aggregations. Alternatively, it is possible to identify a threshold, and only the output is counted if it passes those quality criteria (*e.g.* "the number of passports issued within five working days from receipt of the correct fee and correctly completed application" or "the percentage of financial statement audits opinions that were issued on, or within two days of the signing of the financial statements"). The combination of quality and quantity indicators in one measure is particularly important for SNA calculations. For managerial and policy purposes, this is less of an issue as managers often need a disaggregated view on quality and quantity.

Monitoring and validating performance data

Financial information systems combat misrepresentation by installing extensive internal control systems, supplemented by internal and external audit systems (Raaum and Morgan, 2001; Sterck *et al.*, 2006). As the use and significance of output data increases, similar quality management and quality assurance systems must be used for these. Again, the experience of the over-reliance on output data for planning and control in the Soviet system is salutary. Nove (1958) points out that in that system, since all parties shared the same goals of being seen to be associated with increasing outputs, all were prepared to connive in inflating output reports.

Auditing the quality of the output data and the systems that generate them is a possible strategy to prevent loss of data quality. In the United Kingdom, the majority of Public Service Agreement (PSA) indicators are collected by the departments and agencies themselves.[12] Statistics that are declared valid by the National Statistician and the Statistics Commission receive a National Statistics label. Fourteen percent of the sources of data used for measuring 2001-04 Public Service Agreement targets qualified for this label, but almost half of the departments found that getting assurance on the reliability of performance data is an important challenge (Comptroller and Auditor General, 2001). In 2000, the UK Treasury decided that departments must add a technical note to the PSA, including the technical details of the indicators; however, subsequent studies indicated that departments rarely mentioned how data quality was guaranteed in these technical notes.

Sharman (2001) argued that performance measurement systems should be externally assessed. The UK National Audit Office has undertaken some of this work, in specific value-for-money audits, but does not have a general remit to regularly monitor the whole system of performance information (although the Comptroller and Auditor General has expressed an interest in doing this). When making specific studies of the measurement systems of particular agencies, the National Audit Office looks at three factors (National Audit Office, 2005):

- the match between the performance measure and the data used to report progress;

- data stream operation, including data collection, provision, processing, maintenance and analysis/interpretation; and

- the presentation/reporting of results.

These audits consider both the quality of the internal performance measurement systems of the departments and the quality of the performance information that is reported to Parliament. The purpose of these audits is to assess the risks of data quality limitations. The focus is not on the level of individual indicators, but on the level of performance measurement systems and performance reporting. PSAs are agreed for three years, and measurement systems in departments are audited once during this period.

The Australian National Audit Office (ANAO) does not issue opinions on the non-financial information in the annual report but audits the quality of performance measurement systems within its value-for-money (VFM) audit mandate. For example, the ANAO examined the performance information in the 2000-01 Portfolio Budget Statements of 10 agencies. The ANAO assessed the appropriateness of the performance information in the Portfolio Budget Statements, the reporting of performance information in annual reports and agency arrangements to identify and collect this information. Several difficulties were identified. Outcome indicators were found not to measure outcomes and the targets that were provided were often vague and/or ambiguous. The ANAO advised that minimum Portfolio Budget Statement data quality standards should be established and monitored to ensure that the data supplied to Parliament are valid, reliable and accurate (Australian National Audit Office, 2001).

There has been extensive work on the practical, financial and theoretical limitations of the increasing effort placed on internal regulation and auditing within government (James, 2000). Auditing of output data can be a costly enterprise. The costs involved must be weighed against the benefits in particular areas of application. For planning purposes, auditing is generally not considered necessary. For accountability purposes, auditing may only be worthwhile in particular policy areas.

An alternative approach emphasised by Burgess *et al.* (2002) is to ensure that the data are produced by organisations other than those who must plan or who will be held accountable based on the data.

Bevan and Hood (2006) suggest that one response to gaming is to introduce some degree of randomness into monitoring and evaluation. They note that when targets are defined at a high level of specificity, then there needs to be some uncertainty for those being monitored in how the results are measured. The technical specifications for the outputs (how they are defined in terms of volume and quality) would need to remain constant – but the exact timing and nature of the inspection to verify that reported outputs correspond with actual outputs could vary.

Changing the method of measuring outputs does not imply that the organisational targets are frequently changed. Although there is no value in rigidity, volatility in targets and objectives doubtless creates confusion for agencies and managers, and likely leads to additional costs.

2.2.4. Reducing the incentives for gaming

Although "ownership" is a rather fashionable word with a somewhat ill-defined meaning, there clearly is some significance in ensuring that the managers and agencies responsible for outputs "own" the measures, in the sense that they agree that the measures capture an important aspect of performance and are committed to reporting on them. This is a significant theme of the report of the Public Administration Committee (2003) which argues for detailed proposals for increasing consultation with the producers of government services and with the users of the services. The latter is of course particularly significant if quality measures are designed to reflect the views of users concerning the services.

The connection with the problem of gaming lies in the issue of staff motivation. Without commitment to outputs, staff are more likely to resort to the manipulation of data and/or outputs.[13] One aspect of achieving this staff commitment is to design measures that celebrate progress and identify failure accurately and fairly. The worst case of failing to achieve ownership is to create gamers out of staff who were previously honest and dutiful professionals.

One interesting speculation is that staff are less likely to game if any resulting impact on their reputation matters for their subsequent career. If correct, this would suggest that staff that see their future outside of the civil service might be less inhibited about gaming.[14]

Ultimately, when decisions are driven by output measurement and other sources of information play a negligible role, the incentives for gaming are at their highest. However, when output measurement is one source of information to be incorporated with others, particularly by providing more room for qualitative interpretation and explicit political and managerial judgment, then there is less weight put on a single set of numbers and correspondingly less reason to seek to manipulate them.

2.2.5. Composite indicators – important but risky

A collection of disparate variables on key aspects of the public sector provides both opportunities and challenges for policy makers. How far can these be aggregated into a single index? On the one hand, if each individual variable captures a discrete and narrowly defined concept, then it is relatively straightforward to determine what the variable is describing and consequently the action necessary to change it is reasonably clear. However, on the other hand, a profusion of separate variables gives little indication about the larger reform strategy – each might mean something at the micro-level, but stepping back, they provide a scatter shot picture of developments.

One way around this problem is to accompany the individual variables with composite indicators that aggregate the different components in order to provide a more strategic snapshot of the situation. Ideally, the composite indicators provide the headlines, leading policy makers into a rational debate concerning the drivers of good or bad performance.

There are significant risks in this approach however, very particularly in relation to public management. The primary risk is that the political significance of any measures of public sector performance is such that the debate is more likely to stay at the headline level than to trigger a serious analytic focus on the underlying success factors, problem areas or reform possibilities. Second, there is the significant possibility that such a composite indicator might suggest a spurious degree of precision in inter-country ranking, and could be downright misleading.

The risk of a composite indicator being misleading arises because compiling various variables into a single indicator can disguise some major definitional or conceptual problems. For instance, composite indicators for good governance encounter these problems. Good governance includes several elements – accountability, transparency, corruption. While good governance seems to have an intuitively clear meaning, there are many dimensions (avoidance of conflict of interest, clear public procurement processes, fiscal transparency, public reporting on service delivery standards, etc.) and it is not at all clear whether, or how, these can be combined. If these composite indices are to be used for country comparisons, the contextual nature of good governance has to be taken into account. For instance, improving governance in developing countries is likely to require a different approach to improving governance in developed countries (Schick, 1996).

Aggregation compounds these problems as definitional uncertainties become exacerbated by statistical mixing of apples and oranges, with somewhat arbitrary weightings. As Knack notes: "Aggregate (composite) indexes have no explicit definition, but instead are defined implicitly by what goes into them" (Knack, 2006).[15] At the same time, and most perniciously, aggregation can obscure weaknesses in the underlying data by focusing attention on the aggregation techniques.

Aggregation also brings other risks. It can make it difficult or impossible to track data over time, as the mix of underlying sources is changing. It can also overemphasise particular aspects of a topic, as some of the underlying indicators are interdependent and so are really measuring the same thing. (Nardo *et al.*, 2005) highlight these risks in detail in the *OECD Handbook on Constructing Composite Indicators.*

The appropriate risk mitigation strategy would be to ensure that each composite indicator complies with the criteria set out in Box 2.2.[16]

The most likely area for the development of composite indicators is in narrowly defined categories of public sector processes (degree of openness of human resource management arrangements) or in equally narrow categories of outputs. However, even in these more narrowly defined areas, the risks of composite indicators are not negligible.

2.2.6. The problem of the missing theory

Box 2.2 summarises the steps identified in the OECD Handbook on Constructing Composite Indicators as necessary for the meaningful construction of composite indicators. The binding constraint on the construction of composite indicators is the existence of a clear theoretical framework. This criterion more or less rules out the creation of any composite indicator at the whole-of-government level – as there is simply no agreed framework for evaluating efficiency, effectiveness, accountability or indeed any of a number of other crucial aspects, of overall public sector performance.[17]

Box 2.2 Summary of OECD criteria for constructing composite indicators

- Clear theoretical framework

- Indicators selected on the basis of their quality and relevance

- The methodological choice in weighting and aggregation exposed

- Different approaches for imputing missing values exposed

- Indicators normalised to render them comparable.

- Indicators aggregated and weighted according to the underlying theoretical framework

- Explicit assessments made of the robustness of the composite indicator

- Composite indicator correlated with other data

- Presentation should clarify not mislead

- Underlying indicators or values should be readily available

Source: Developed from Nardo *et al.* (2005).

Box 2.3 sets out one way to simplify some of the reasons for public sector reform. OECD (2005c) emphasises that the weight given to each institutional reform or outcome varies by country and over time. In sum, these might be widely prevalent objectives, but there is certainly no common framework for determining how much they matter or for whom. There is no prospect of any defensible single aggregate measure that would show overall public sector performance improvements, as there is no agreement on what such improvements comprise.

Box 2.3 Some dimensions of public sector reform

The recent OECD review of public sector modernisation (2005c) provides an overview of the key features of recent institutional changes within government. The review highlights the multiplicity of objectives in recent reforms. At the level of institutions and structures, the review notes that reforms have entailed refinements to the mechanisms:

- for accountability and control (changes in internal and external control, and developments in public reporting)

- for preparing and executing the budget (developments in fiscal rules, strengthened emphasis on medium-term perspectives and enhanced budget transparency) and

- for public employment and management (delegation of establishment control, recruitment and human resource management, decentralised wage bargaining, personalised contracts and individual responsibility for careers, and performance management with stronger monetary and career incentives).

The review also notes that these have been driven by concerns to improve key outcomes:

- openness (Freedom of Information improvements, charters and e-government, improved consultation and strengthened offices of the ombudsman)

- agility (strengthening the weight assigned to local and user preferences through decentralisation, clearer market signals through contracting and user charges, and diversification of agency forms in order to provide a focus on service output) and

- quality and efficiency (through stronger mechanisms to motivate individual and agency performance and to highlight the outputs sought through the budget process).

This point is emphasised in an authoritative review of 10 OECD member countries (Pollitt and Bouckaert, 2004). The review identifies 10 frequent objectives of public management reform, which may be in tension or even conflict with each other. These include increase political control vs. free managers to manage vs. empower service consumers, and improve quality vs. cut costs (Pollitt and Bouckaert, 2004). Any attempted theoretical framework for composite indicators would have to justify choices concerning which side of the trade-off wins, and the balance between these objectives. Whilst justifying such trade-offs may sometimes be possible and understandable at the level of an individual service, it is an insurmountable task when addressed at the level of entire public sectors, partly because of the sheer variety of goods and services they are responsible for.[18]

There is scope for some experimentation of course – as long as the results are regarded as a contribution to the debate and not as an authoritative reading on the "real" state of public management reform. Such experimentation is probably best not undertaken by the OECD as this could suggest an inappropriate degree of finality about the conclusions. The components of a proposed "Index of Reform Capacity" by the Bertelsmann Foundation, distinguishing between process objectives (such as accountability of the executive to Parliament, accountability of political parties, capacity to formulate structural and policy reforms, etc.) and outcomes (participation in the electoral process, education levels, etc.) are an interesting example of how such trial measures could be developed (Fischer *et al.*, 2006).

2.3. The risks of non-use and of absent or weak data

We have spent some time above considering the risks involved in performance measurement. To complete this section, however, it is also necessary to consider the risks of not developing and using high quality comparative performance data. Some of the key points are discussed below.

2.3.1. Over-claiming on "best practice"

The paucity of reliable data has, to date, deterred significant progress in the analyses of public sector efficiency and effectiveness as well as institutional effectiveness. Benchmarking and practitioner dialogue have tended to resort to assertions concerning "best practice", with frequent comments that policy fashion has dictated many recent changes.

Many commentators point out that, in the absence of data, belief counts as much as evaluations. "… what we are dealing with here is best described as a kind of religion … a system of belief founded on faith and (which) therefore should not be analysed as though it were some kind of body of scientific knowledge subject to objective tests" (Pollitt and Bouckaert, 2003). The same commentators point out that, remarkably, this lack of robust data has not diminished the certainty of reformers: "There is something of a paradox at the heart of the international movement in favour of performance-oriented management reform. The reformers insist that public sector organisations must reorient and reorganise themselves in order to focus more vigorously on their results. They must count costs, measure outputs, assess outcomes, and use all this information in a systematic process of feedback and continuous improvement. Yet this philosophy has clearly not been applied to many of the reforms themselves, which have thus far been evaluated relatively seldom, and usually in ways that have some serious methodological limitations …" (Pollitt and Bouckaert, 2004).[19]

These concerns about inappropriately enthusiastic and uncritical acceptance of managerial and policy reforms are echoed within more specialist areas such as the health sector, where Marmor *et al.* (2005) find that: "There is … a considerable gap between promise and performance in the field of comparative policy studies. Misdescription and superficiality are all too common. Unwarranted inferences, rhetorical distortion, and caricatures – all show up too regularly in comparative health policy scholarship and debates." They conclude that "(p)erhaps the most important lesson we can draw from the overview in the current literature is that the development of a serious body of comparative work takes more time and effort than health policy makers are willing to spend. They feel pressures to take action and feel they cannot wait. At the same time, policy errors based on misconceptions of the experience abroad can be costly" (Marmor *et al.*, 2005).

It is, however, worth noting that reforms are undertaken for many more reasons than just efficiency and effectiveness. The need to shake up a seemingly moribund administration and political interest in being seen to take charge of a sector or an issue play their parts (Pollitt and Bouckaert, 2003).

2.3.2. Short institutional memories

A review of developments in executive agencies in the United Kingdom (Talbot and Johnson, 2006) points out that in 1988, the UK central government embarked on what has become one of the most quoted emblematic cases of disaggregation – the break-up of the previously monolithic civil service into "executive agencies" as a result of the "Next Steps" Report. As a result of the reforms, the UK central government moved from having around 17 ministries to, by the mid-1990s, having roughly the same number of ministries plus at one point nearly 130 executive agencies or organisations "working on Next Steps lines". This was seemingly impressive change and was widely cited and emulated in something of an "agency fever". The review suggests that in 2006 the picture is very different. From the large-scale disaggregation of the early 1990s, policy seems to have been significantly reversed itself, with the number of civil servants working in agencies having dropped from its high of 75% to just over 53% at most, and most likely to only 38%.

Similarly, a recent review of US government reforms suggests that "the deluge of recent reform may have done little to actually improve performance. On the contrary, it may have created confusion within government about what Congress and the President really want, distraction from needed debates about organisational missions and resources, and the illusion that more reform will somehow lead to better government" (Light, 2006).

Others might strongly challenge these propositions. However, with such limited time series data, it is all but impossible to determine the degree to which such alleged reversals or reform overloads have occurred.

2.3.3. Limited understanding of possibilities for improving efficiency or effectiveness

In the search for efficiency measures, the work by Porta *et al.* (1998) illustrates the dilemma that researchers find themselves in, given the weak state of data. The authors assessed government performance using measures of government intervention, public sector efficiency, public good provision, size of government, and political freedom. Many of these data were at a very aggregate level and included composite indicators constructed from primarily perception-based data.[20] The finding that, *inter alia*, countries that use French laws exhibit inferior government performance is, to say the least, contestable.

More recently, a much publicised European Central Bank publication concluded that "countries with lean public sectors and public expenditure ratios not far from 30% of GDP tend to be most efficient" and that "countries could use around 45% less resources to attain the same outcomes if they were fully efficient. Average output scores suggest that countries are only delivering around two-thirds of the output they could deliver if they were on the efficiency frontier" (Afonso *et al.*, 2006). Again, given the data and the reliance on composite indicators drawing on perception-based data, the results can be challenged.

On institutional effectiveness, to the degree that there is a common goal amongst OECD member countries of economic stability combined with low poverty, then the analysis by the Social and Cultural Planning Office (2004) highlights that the current data can support few conclusions beyond the obvious points that history and culture matter.[21] Certainly, no conclusions can be drawn concerning the relationship between these outcomes and institutional design within the public sector.

Notes

1. "(P)erformance measurement is the quantitative representation through measurement of the quality or quantity of input, output, and/or outcome of organisations or programs in its societal context" (Sterck *et al.*, 2006).

2. In the last 50 years, the System of National Accounts became one of the most institutionalised measurement systems in society. Although the conceptual development can be traced back to the 17th century, the global institutional development is a post-war phenomenon (Bos, 2003).

3. Benchmarking comprises: "(t)wo or more participants making systematic comparisons of processes and/or results in their respective organisations in order to learn about best practices and implement them in ways suited to their own organisation" (European Institution of Public Administration, 2002). "Benchmarking is a method for improving performance by identifying, understanding, comparing, and adapting one's own organization with the outstanding practices and processes of others" (United States Department of Defense, undated). See also Aulnck (2002).

4   "(A)t its simplest, benchmarking means: 'Improving ourselves by learning from others' … 'Benchmarking is simply about making comparisons with other organisations and then learning the lessons that those comparisons throw up'. Source: The European Benchmarking Code of Conduct" (The UK Public Sector Benchmarking Service:
    http://www.benchmarking.gov.uk/about bench/whatisit.asp).

5. See for example: Institute for Citizen-Centred Service (*http://www.iccs-isac.org/eng/bench-ben.htm*) and Treasury Board Management Accountability Framework (*http://www.tbs-sct.gc.ca/maf-crg/documents/booklet-livret/booklet-livret_e.pdf*).

6. Public sector reform trajectories are also identified as significant to understanding the likelihood of reform success in developing countries (International Monetary Fund and World Bank, 2006). It is possible that, over time, analysis of such paths might throw some light on a key evaluation question – what is the counter-factual? What would have happened if the reform had not been implemented? (Boston, 2000).

7. There is a very extensive empirically-based literature on this topic. It is well-surveyed in Van Dooren (2006).

8. Behn and Kant (1999) and Grizzle (2002) describe this as cream skimming (or cherry picking) – easy cases and clients are processed while the more difficult cases are redirected. Smith (1995) also identifies the risk that excessively rigid

measurement system may lead to organisational paralysis, with a fear of experimentation.

9.   Bouckaert and Balk (1991) use a variety of medical metaphors to describe these issues. Gaming might include the public sector equivalent of hypertrophy (an enlargement of overgrowth of an organ due to an increase in the size of its constituent cells) where measurement causes the volume or quantity of a specific output to be increased because it is measured. They also identify atrophy when non-measured or hard to measure qualitative aspects of outputs are reduced. Bouckaert (1995) refers to myopia when the long-term view is excluded by a fixation on short-term measurement-driven goals, and tunnel vision, when organisations only pay attention to those activities that are being measured, with associated pursuit of local organisational objectives at the expense of larger government objectives (Bouckaert and Balk, 1991; Hood: 1974; Perrin, 1998).

10.   Propper and Wilson (2003) provides a useful summary of the perverse incentives in health and education in the United Kingdom and in the United States.

11.   As an example of an early alert, Atkinson *et al.* (2005) notes, in relation to the UK Department of Welfare and Pensions (DWP) Public Service Agreement (PSA) targets that "(t)he current measure fails to register important dimensions of quality of service such as accuracy of claims, turnaround time, and the reduction of fraud. It does not assess whether DWP is adding value in respect of its wider PSA objectives, in respect of social security or labour market and other functions."

12.   The UK developed a system of Public Service Agreements (see: *http://www.hm-treasury.gov.uk/spending_review/spend_sr04/psa/spend_sr04_psaindex.cfm*).
Before these agreements are published they are negotiated with the Treasury as part of Spending Reviews, taking account of costs. Line ministers are held accountable through a statement of responsibility (as part of the Public Service Agreement) that explicitly names them as being responsible for delivering the PSA. They are, additionally, held accountable through the discussion of reports on the realisation of public service commitments in Parliament, and past performance is taken into account when negotiating departmental budgets with the Treasury.

13.   Bevan and Hood (2005) make this point in their characterisation of potential gamers as: saints, honest triers, reactive gamers and rational maniacs.

14.   Point raised by Oliver James, University of Exeter.

15.   See also Knack *et al.* (2003); Sudders and Nahem (2004); Van de Walle (2005).

16.   See
*http://www.oecd.org/document/35/0,2340,en_2649_33735_38218595_1_1_1_1,
00.html*

17.   It is important to note that this problem of constructing a composite index at the level of the overall public sector does not amount to a proposition that there have been no performance improvements – either in individual countries over time, or in the OECD as a whole. It does however lead to the proposition that, in the current state of the art, there is little to be gained and perhaps much to be lost in claiming that at this level it is possible to move beyond practitioner anecdotes to a more scientific basis.

18.   The recent development of many and various aggregate measures of "governance" has not solved the problem (see discussion above on governance indicators). The underlying uncertainties embodied in current academic theories are set out well in (Boyne *et al.*, 2003).

19.   Similar points are made by Hood (2005) and Pollitt (1995).

20.   For example, an indicator of government efficiency was constructed with perception-based data from the International Country Risk Guide (ICRG), Business Environmental Risk Intelligence's (BERI) Operation Risk Index and the Global Competitiveness Report 1996. It also included public sector employment data which are fraught with definitional problems.

21.   The Social and Cultural Planning Office (2004) constructed composite indicators for economic stability from growth rate in GDP, unemployment rate, inflation and budget deficits/surplus as a percentage of GDP. Using that indicator, they showed that the Central European countries show moderate economic stability (particularly in terms of inflation, unemployment and the budget deficit), but also a low poverty rate. The Western and Northern European countries are generally characterised by a fairly positive score for both criteria. The Southern European countries as a rule score fairly negatively on both criteria. The English-speaking countries, including the United Kingdom, have moderate economic stability and a high poverty rate.

Chapter 3. Output Measurement: Key Issues

Governments need to measure inputs, processes, outputs and outcomes. To argue for better and more extensive measurement of outputs is in no way to dismiss or deny the need for other kinds of measures. Nevertheless, outputs have a special place. They are in a sense the final products of public sector organisations – what the organisation delivers to its users – the license, grant, surgical procedure, school lesson, pension or prison sentence. So they are, usually, what elected representatives and the public can actually hold those organisations responsible for. Furthermore, they are things which we can reasonably expect those organisations to keep track of themselves – we can expect them to know how many lessons/grants/licenses, etc. they are producing, at what cost, and with what quality.

Thus, despite many uncertainties in the relationship between public sector outputs and objectives or agreed outcomes, the measurement of outputs is fundamental to any empirical understanding of public sector performance. However, internationally there is an extensive and continuing debate about how to measure outputs and how to use the measurements to influence individual, agency and overall public sector behaviour:

> We considered whether, in the light of the evidence of professional demoralisation, perverse consequences, unfair pressure and alleged cheating, the culture of measurement should be swept away. Should there be a cull of targets and tables to allow the front line to work unhindered by central direction?

> This is a superficially attractive prospect, but an unrealistic and undesirable one. The increases in accountability and transparency brought about by the last twenty years of performance measurement have been valuable. Information is now available that cannot and must not be suppressed. Open government demands that people have the right to know how well their services are being delivered, and professionals and managers need to be held to account. The aim must be to build on these developments, while reducing any negative effects.

> OECD Public Administration Select Committee (2003)

One key constraint to developing a balanced picture of developments in output measurement is the limited availability of literature and experiences from non English-speaking countries, other than the extensive work in the Nordic countries (particularly Finland and Sweden) and the Netherlands. Here we draw on practitioner comments,[1] commissioned papers (Van Dooren *et al.*, 2006) and reviews of OECD experiences (OECD, 2005b), to attempt to correct this otherwise somewhat skewed picture.

3.1. Technical issues

3.1.1. Transaction vs. provision

Perhaps the most fundamental technical distinction is between output measures that capture transactions, and those that reflect the provision of services. Transactional approaches, mostly adopted by economists, count output when the transaction is complete, *i.e.* when the output is consumed. The provision approach, mostly adopted by the public administration discipline, sees output as products or services that come out of a democratically supervised production process, regardless of whether they are consumed or not. Instead of the number of pupils or prisoners, the number of teaching hours or the number of cells are defined as the outputs.

This distinction is relevant for the politically vital question of holding people or entities to account. The organisations that are providing services often can have no impact or only limited impact on the level of consumption. For example, prisons cannot reasonably be held accountable for the decreasing prison population if, fortuitously, criminality decreases. But they can be held to account for the quality and cost of their services, and for the conformity of services with goals and standards laid down in policy. This approach therefore stresses issues of accountability, transparency, and accessibility, as well as those of technical efficiency. All these dimensions can, in different ways, be subject to measurement. The production/provision perspective thus links with some of the key themes of the OECD's recent overview, *Modernising Government: The Way Forward* (2005).

3.1.2. Easy to measure vs. hard to measure

There is a sense amongst many practitioners as well as academics that some activities are easier to measure than others (for an overview, see Bouckaert and Halachmi, 1995). The nature of the output differs between organisations. In organisations undertaking tasks with a high degree of ambiguity and low standardisation, such as embassies and cultural institutions, measurement of output is of course more difficult. By contrast, public housing corporations are a typical example of a sector with less ambiguity and more routine/standardised forms of provision. Wilson (1989) proposes a distinction between four types of organisations: production, procedural, craft and coping organisations, based on whether their output and outcome can be observed or not.[2] Output measurement will be easier in production and procedural organisations and more difficult in craft and coping organisations. Wilson argues that these features have strong implications for the most appropriate ways of leading and managing such organisations.

Summarising this debate, it is clear that some outputs are less susceptible to measurement (as summarised in Figure 3.1) and will require more effort to obtain high-quality measures. Efforts to obtain information need to be in balance with the potential benefits of acquiring the information. An important consideration in this respect is the question of how important financially and socially the output happens to be. For example, measuring the output of overseas embassies is probably at the hard to measure end of the spectrum. At the same time, it is perhaps not that financially important or a central subject of political/social debate. Therefore, it is sensible for governments not to devote huge amounts of time to this enterprise. On the other hand, measuring health service output properly is also difficult. However, it is socially and financially enormously important and so efforts must be made to find meaningful measures.

Figure 3.1. Ease of output measurement

Easy to measure ⟵⟶	Hard to measure
low ambiguity highly routinised	high ambiguity low level of routine
production tasks procedure-based operations	craft tasks coping organisations

Source: Developed from Van Dooren *et al.* (2006).

The implications for measurement design are that for hard to measure outputs, proxies, subjective judgments and discursive ("tin-opener") approaches are more likely to be necessary. This is not intrinsically fatal to any attempts at measuring the output, but it certainly implies some more caution, discussion and experimentation.

Difficulties in measurability can be compounded when goods and services are grouped together. Output measures often represent an attempt to capture a bundle of goods and services. Residential care, for example, entails a complex package of services including the provision of meals, infrastructure, nursing and psychological support. The apparent ease of measurement of the aggregate package might be concealing significant difficulties in measurement within some of the constituent components. The aggregation of different measures within composite indices is a particularly risky step, which should only be undertaken with great caution and clarity concerning weightings and the "meaning" of the resulting index.

3.1.3. Individual vs. collective

The traditional economic classification of services makes a distinction between individual and collective goods and services. The distinction between individual and collective goods arises from whether the consumption of one person rivals that of another and whether exclusion of third persons is feasible or not (Musgrave and Musgrave, 1984).

The individual/collective distinction is often conflated with the easy to measure/hard to measure distinction. It can be argued that individual services are on average easier to measure than collective services. However, averages may conceal substantial differences. As is shown in Table 3.1, examples of collective and individual public goods can be found with both low and high measurability. Measurability is an important concept for developing a measurement agenda. It determines, amongst others, whether ambitions of measurement efforts are realistic. The use of the individual/collective distinction as a proxy for measurability may lead to unrealistic expectations.

Table 3.1 Functional classification versus measurability

		Functional classification	
		Collective (public goods)	Individual (merit goods)
Measurability	Low	National defence	Job counselling
	High	Road construction	Vehicle registration

Note: Strictly speaking, merit goods are goods that are determined by government to be good for people, regardless of whether people desire them for themselves or not. This is not exactly the same as individual goods.

Source: Van Dooren *et al.* (2006).

3.2. Utilisation

Given that the achievement of outcome targets cannot be attributed to single sector-specific government actions, it is not surprising that recent

OECD surveys indicate that in the budget process, outcome measures are used considerably less than output measures. When OECD senior budget official representatives were asked in 2005 about the types of performance measures that they had developed in relation to the budget process, half of the respondents said that they tracked data that combined output and outcomes. Over a third indicated that they (also) tracked the unit cost of outputs as a performance measure. About ten per cent said that they collected output data only (Curristine, 2005). Only around three per cent indicated that they used outcome measures alone. The responses were not mutually exclusive.

That said, it is important not to overstate the degree to which the direct measures of the volume of government output cover all of government activity. In the United Kingdom, a major proponent of direct output measurement for the SNA, direct estimates now cover some two-thirds of general government final consumption (Atkinson *et al.*, 2005). In other OECD member countries, the proportion of government activity captured by output measures is likely to be a lot smaller. This reflects a lack of consensus on the technical feasibility of output measurement, and an associated resistance to over concentrating on the service delivery role of government at the expense of the harder to measure activities such as regulation and policy development, etc.

This might be changing in some settings however. The UK Comptroller and Auditor General (2001) demonstrates the changing balance between these categories of performance measures in the United Kingdom. Public Service Agreement targets during the period 1999-2002 were categorised as: inputs (7%); process (51%); outputs (27%); outcomes (15%). During the period 2001-04, they were categorised as: inputs (5%); process (14%); outputs (13%); outcomes (68%).[3] Arguably, there is a trade-off between the attention given to output and outcome measures – and so the increased focus on outcomes has a price.

3.2.1. Key relationships

Broadly, there are five key relationships that entail the use of output measures. They appear in the various documents, agreements and laws as shown in Table 3.2.

Table 3.2 Use of output indicators (excluding contracts subject to judicial enforcement)

Parties involved	*Ex ante*	*Ex post*
1. Individual – manager	Appointment discussions Performance agreements	Performance assessments
2. Work unit/agency – line minister	Strategic plan/corporate plan Business plan Unit performance plan Service level agreements	Annual reports Quality control and inspection
3. Line minister – Minister of Finance	Estimates in appropriations bills Public service agreements and commitments	Public accounts Public service delivery reports
4. Line minister – Parliament	Estimates in appropriation bills Policy statements Public service agreements and commitments	Public accounts Public service delivery reports
5. Government – community/wider public	Citizen-driven performance measurement	Citizen-driven performance measurement League tables, citizens' charters Output reporting in the National Accounts (section 3)

Notes: Particularly in English-speaking countries, emphasis is laid on the commitments of service delivery agencies, and the ministers responsible for them, towards government as a whole and to the public. In the United Kingdom these commitments are known as Public Service Agreements (see: *www.hm-treasury.gov.uk/spending_review/spend_sr04/psa/spend_sr04_psaindex.cfm*).

For each relationship, output measures can contribute to a planning[4] discussion or can be employed in actions concerned with accountability and control.[5] The former commences a discussion on policy alternatives or a reflection on past actions, in which some or many factors are not immediately clear and not included in the output measure. Generally, the latter entails sanctions or incentive schemes and therefore too much leeway for interpretation is problematic.

At each level, there is an extensive debate underway as to the appropriate uses of the measures, their technical merits and defects, and the risks of "gaming".

Individual – manager

The new public management conception of a quasi-contractual principal-agent relationship between employee and manager has had a strong influence on recent human resource management reforms within the public sector. Performance measures for individuals include a significant component of output measurement of individual effort. Some key elements of a somewhat confusing practitioner debate include on the one hand concerns about the perverse impact of performance targets and the alleged over-emphasis on the measurable at the expense of traditional values and ethics, encouraging short-sighted gaming for personal career advantage. On the other, there is a concern that without such measures, public employees will lack clear guidance on expectations and service provision will become inevitably captured by provider interests.

Performance expectations, including the capacity of the staff member to deliver specified outputs based on track record, can be considered during appointment discussions, and this can be seen as a planning discussion concerning the individual's anticipated contribution. However, performance assessments can entail the use of output measures and relate to performance sanctions and rewards.

Work unit/agency – line minister

At the level of the work unit or agency, output measures inform the various business plans. However, it is recognised that these plans must also take into account other unmeasurable or unpredictable factors. Various types of service level agreements entail output measures and contribute to planning and budgeting discussions. All are duly offered for ministerial and wider review in various forms of annual reports. Failure to deliver the outputs indicated in the plans and service level agreements normally would not form the basis for automatic budgetary rewards or sanctions. This is because, while poor performance clearly calls for political and managerial attention, it is not clear whether deteriorating output performance points towards an increase or a decrease in budgetary allocations.

In general there are different traditions in OECD member countries concerning oversight procedures vis-à-vis work units/agencies. The Scandinavian model leans strongly on surveillance of work units/agencies by policy making units in the core ministries; the English-speaking Commonwealth model leans more on surveillance by central support bodies in the core ministries (mainly the financial directorates of the ministries).

Output agreements between work units/agencies and ministers are to a certain degree comparable to contracts in the private service sector. Such contracts are always incomplete contracts in that outputs are not fully described at the time of initial agreement and that they allow the principal to intervene during contract execution and further specify the outputs within broad conditions established in the initial contract (Williamson, 1975; Pollitt *et al.*, 2004).

Line minister – Minister of Finance

Output measures can be the base for the annual bilateral exercise in which the (multi-annual) estimates are adjusted or extended. Thus output estimates contribute towards planning discussions. Within public accounts they have an accountability purpose but again, despite the current emphasis on "performance" within the budget process, in practice output measures provide little or no basis for automatic budgetary rewards or sanctions. In this case, in addition to the conceptual problem mentioned, any such usage would also presuppose a very strong Minister of Finance able to punish in some way defaulting ministries. Governments in OECD member countries generally do not provide the Minister of Finance with this degree of authority (Hallerberg and Von Hagen, 1997; Von Hagen, 1992). In general, the only thing that the Minister of Finance can realistically sanction is the budgetary effects of policy changes that are incompatible with the budget or prevailing multi-year envelopes.

Line minister – Parliament

This is a crucial relationship for the discussion of outputs. Ministers make plans for their ministries partly in terms of outputs and can be held accountable for them in Parliament (and in the public discussion with civil society – see below). These are stated as the basis for the Appropriation Acts or Budget Bills, budget statements and any PSAs reported to Parliament. Thus, Parliament could in principle use output measures to trigger any sanctions that it wishes to apply. However, failure to deliver output targets would form the basis for a discussion which, however ominous, would not amount to an automatic sanction. It should also be noted that the evidence thus far is that legislatures frequently make only very limited use of the performance information that they are provided with (Pollitt, 2006).

Government – community/wider public

The use of output measures in the relationship between government in general and the wider public is most readily associated with "naming and shaming" through "League Tables", "Citizen Charters" and the like. In some countries, such as the United Kingdom, the data collection and publication of such information is considered as a task of government. In other countries, such as Germany and the Netherlands, such information is mainly published by consumer organisations and the media. In the case of competitive markets for such information, different providers might publish different results, based on different conceptions of quality and different criteria and measurement methods. The agency output measures that attract public attention are those that are the most consistent with the idea of citizens' or customers' rights to a particular level or quality of service.

Box 3.1 Providing output information to Parliament in Australia and the United Kingdom

In Australia, the Appropriation Bill is structured around the outcomes that the government wants to achieve for each portfolio. This implies that Parliament appropriates resources for results. The outcomes in the Appropriation Bills are formulated in very broad terms.

The portfolio budget statements then provide additional details and explanations of the budget to inform members of Parliament and the public of the proposed allocation of resources to government outcomes. The portfolio budget statements specify the price, quality and quantity of outputs that agencies will deliver and the criteria they will use for demonstrating the contribution of agency outputs and administered items to outcomes (Chan *et al.*, 2002). The portfolio budget statement is formulated by the portfolio department in consultation with the agencies involved.

Departments report every year in September on their activities and performance by means of an annual report. This annual report includes the financial statements and a performance report that gives an overview of the achievements against the objectives set out in the portfolio budget statement. In the financial statements, costs are linked to outcomes and outputs. The notes to the financial statements include, for example, information on the total cost per outcome and the revenues and expenses per output group.

In the United Kingdom, the spending of government departments is normally authorised by Parliament by means of an Appropriation Act. Departmental spending plans are broken down into one or more "requests for resources", which are structured along the broad objectives of the government.

More specific targets for a number of services are set by means of PSAs, negotiated between the Treasury and the line department. The PSAs set out the targets that departments should work to meet while keeping within their three-year fixed departmental expenditure limits (although some PSA targets have a life-span beyond the three years of the Spending Review). The budgets and targets are reviewed during the Spending Review (usually every two years).

Departments report on their activities and achievement by means of a Departmental Report that is usually published in the spring. This report provides Parliament and the public with an account of how the department has spent the resources allocated to it, as well as its future spending plans. It also describes the different policies and programmes and gives a breakdown of spending within these programmes, in addition to reporting progress on PSAs.

In the late autumn, departments have to report a second time on the progress against PSA targets. Autumn Performance Reports were introduced in 2002 to supplement reporting against PSA targets in Departmental Reports. The report is published in late autumn and highlights progress towards achieving the PSA targets following the progress reports in the Departmental Report in April.

In the United Kingdom, non-financial information is also included in the financial statements. The net operating costs are linked to the departmental objectives in Schedule 5: Statement of Resources by Aims and Objectives. Schedule 5 makes the actual costs of the different departmental objectives transparent.

In general, this is a very indirect form of accountability as there are no immediate or direct consequences for the agencies or programmes. Accountability via public reporting of output information is most common in relation to the English-speaking countries, where this form of accountability is strong (Ammons, 2003; Dubnik, 1998). "League Tables", "Citizen Charters" and various forms of annual reporting are examples of this accountability role (Gormley and Weimer, 1999).

However, where a quasi-market has been established, such as in the UK education system, potential consumers can be provided with information on the outputs of various service providers and, to the extent that resources follow the customer, this information can trigger a more direct form of sanctioning. However, under no circumstance is this form of sanctioning comparable to that in private sector markets and is never automatic. Sanctioning through consumer choice is always dependent on the assessment of information by the individual consumer. The consumer may maintain trust in spite of unfavourable output information and he/she may lose trust in spite of favourable output information. Output information is one factor among others which determines assessment and sanctioning. Even in the absence of quasi markets, media attention for bad performers will definitely put pressure on politicians "to do something". The second order consequences, through markets or politicians, may be even more far reaching then the more direct accountability mechanisms.[6]

3.2.2. Planning and control/accountability

The distinction between the use of output measures for planning and for control and for accountability arises because of the different nature of the incentives that are at stake (Van Dooren, 2005, 2006). Accountability emphasises "sticks" while planning and service improvement suggest "carrots". In both areas output measures are usually only loosely connected to decisions.

The Public Administration Select Committee of the UK House of Commons refers to these two areas of application (planning versus accountability) as two cultures of measurement with "high" and "low" pressure" (Public Administration Select Committee, 2003). In their view, high pressure uses are measurement driven and primarily concern accountability. Low pressures uses are primarily for planning purposes and emphasise a loose coupling between the measures and the final decisions.

There is a need, however, to be careful with the connotations of language here. In English "loose coupling" can sound weak and undesirable. But in the debate over indicators there should be no prior assumption that tight coupling is better than loose coupling. Much depends on the context –

including the particular aims of the policy makers and the specific characteristics of the activity. Tight coupling can be problematic if applied to a complex task that is delivered by semi-autonomous professionals. It can lead to de-motivation and high levels of gaming – and to downright perverse results (Bevan and Hood, 2006). In some ways a better terminology would be the one used earlier between indicators as "dials" and indicators as "tin openers" (Carter *et al.*, 1992).

Table 3.3 Use of output measures

Features of the measures	Use of output measures	
	Planning – learning	Control – accountability
Question being addressed	What can we expect? How can we do better?	What is to be delivered? Was it delivered?
Purpose	Formulation of targets Allocation of resources	Settling the bill
Impact on actors	Low pressure	High pressure

Source: Van Dooren *et al.* (2006).

3.2.3. Relating measure design and use

Use of output measures in decision-making

Output measures contribute to decision-making in different ways, with varying degrees of risk concerning gaming:

- Tight: output measurement leads to the decision in a direct way. Decisions are driven mainly by output measurement. Other sources of information play a negligible role.

- Loose: output measurement is one source of information to be incorporated with others. Other sources of information are used to interpret the output measurement data and decisions are informed by output measurement, but also by other sources of information such as experience, qualitative information, etc.

In planning, output measures and consequent predictions are used to facilitate an overall interpretation of which way to go and how to get there. They are provided to facilitate strategic deliberations, but rarely mechanically drive them. This forward looking use of output measures can be intended to improve both services and broader policies (Scheirer, 1994).

There are two reasons why planning for government agencies is generally only loosely connected to output measures. First, agency plans must cover a lot more than just a commitment to produce a certain volume of goods and services. Ultimately, government is concerned with outcomes, and the goods and services that it must deliver to achieve these cannot be predicted with absolute certainty. Locking a commitment about output volumes into the plan would undermine any flexibility necessary to deal with contextual changes. Second, it would have little meaning for funding purposes as it would not be evident from any failure to deliver the outputs whether this was because of an efficiency problem (in which case logical options include either restructuring or having the service provided by a different agency or outsourced) or a problem of under-estimating costs.

Similarly, in control and accountability, output realisations are in practice generally only loosely connected with sanctioning decisions. While output measures can be used to compare deliverables precisely against the commitments that were made, this is not to say that underperformance as revealed by output measurements automatically leads to sanctions when used for accountability. Rather, the measures form the basis for a discussion concerning the failure to meet targets – although of course such a discussion can itself be something of a sanction.[7]

As Table 3.4 indicates, there is a matrix of possibilities.

Table 3.4 The uses of output measures and their contribution to decision-making

| | | Type of decision-making | |
		A. Planning	B. Accountability and control
Relationship between output measures and decision-making	1. Tight (Driven mainly by output measures)	A1. Tight relationship between measures and decisions. Technically and politically difficult use of output measures – gaming likely to be a concern.	B1. Tight relationship between measures and consequences. Strong enforcement effect from output measures – but undermined by encouraging gaming.
	2. Loose (Informed by output measures, but other measures significantly taken into account)	A2. Loose coupling between measures and plans. Very common use – but the impact of output measures can be diluted.	B2. Loose consequence between measures and consequences. When used as the basis for discussions, output measures have a weaker enforcement effect – but gaming can be mitigated.

In planning decisions, output measures can drive the decision, but as cell A1 indicates, this is often a difficult use of such measures. Performance budgeting rhetoric often aspires to this use, impelled by the notion that targets for outputs can always steer the allocation of resources. In practice this is unlikely to succeed for several reasons. As was noted earlier, many government objectives are not measurable in terms of outputs (foreign policy, defence, etc.). There is also a political problem if the motivation of budget estimates in terms of output targets is accompanied by the suppression of input information (wages, various forms of intermediate consumption, etc.), as has sometimes been the case. In Australia, performance budgeting reforms were initiated in order to facilitate discussions on outputs and even outcomes in Parliament. Yet, the output and outcome information that was provided by the departments was very broad whereas input information was reduced. As a result, Parliament felt that it lost some control over the executive branch (Van Dooren and Sterck, 2006).

In addition, to the extent that the measures directly affect real resources, strong incentives for gaming are created. The problems of using transaction data to drive planning were recognised by Charles Goodhart when he light-heartedly offered his "Law" following his analysis of the consequences of the UK government relying solely on money supply targets in the 1970s: "Any observed regularity will tend to collapse once pressure is placed on it for control purposes" (Goodhart, 1975).

As cell A2 indicates, planning decisions can also be loosely or not at all coupled to output measures. This will generally be the case in all policy areas where no good output indicators are available or where objectives can only partly be described by output indicators. In these areas more qualitative target statements as well as tacit knowledge and experience are all factored into these decisions. In "mixed areas" the risk of course is that the arithmetic implications of the output changes can be lost in a sea of other considerations.

In considering accountability and control, as cell B1 suggests, a tight relationship between measures and consequences is theoretically possible. Some applications are allegedly based on this logic, although in practice other considerations may come into play if results are manifestly unreasonable. In human resource management, performance-related pay links a bonus to a quantitative target which is often based on outputs. In performance contracts and service level agreements, the provider is evaluated based on whether the promised performance is achieved or not. However, although such a tight relationship between output measures and control/accountability decisions is feasible, as was noted above it is a distinctly risky venture. Arguably, this is illustrated in the UK-style league tables. In these, the evaluation of the service quality is, in effect, undertaken by individual citizens who decide to go or not to a particular hospital or school and thus output measurements are the only data included in the decision about how the entity is rated. Organisations often feel that they are treated unfairly as a result, because other sources of information are not included in this accountability decision.

In cell B2, there is a loose relationship between output measurement and control/accountability decisions. In this case the measures have a weaker enforcement effect, but can be used as the basis for an accountability discussion that can itself lead to enforcement action. The risk of course is that the accountability discussion becomes little more than a professional conversation with few incentives or sanctions. This is the explicit intention of loosely connected output measures in the benchmarking circles in Germany, the Netherlands and Canada. In these initiatives, output measurement is used to feed into an intentionally general discussion on how organisations are doing. Ideally, the organisations formulate trajectories for improvement at the end of the process.

The tradeoffs between cells B1 and B2 makes it clear that careful consideration needs to be given on the one hand to whether the risks of gaming ensuing from a tight relationship between output measures and accountability decisions outweighs the benefits of the strong enforcement effect. On the other hand, there is the risk that the gains from reduced gaming are less significant than the losses from the rather light enforcement effect of using output measures as the basis for a discussion. In situations where there serious "life or death" consequences attached to output measurement, there will almost always be a tight coupling. Numbers are more difficult to legally contest compared to other sources of information such as qualitative descriptions of substandard performance.

Relationship between the basis of output measures and their use

Prima facie, the design of output measures is likely to have some significance in relation to the intended use of the data for planning or for accountability and control.

The transaction (consumption) approach to the measurement of outputs can give an indication of the distribution of the output in society. When these data are combined with overall socio-demographic data that identify the need, they are useful for planning purposes as they can give an idea about the adequacy of the output. The disadvantage of the transaction approach is that the number of transactions is often determined by factors outside of government's reach, *e.g.* socio-demographic change. A pure comparison of the number of transactions will thus often mainly reflect this socio-demographic change and not the functioning of government, and so their use for accountability purposes is more limited. An agency that pays unemployment benefits cannot be held accountable for the volume of benefits paid, as this is largely driven by economic factors. It can be held accountable for providing the capacity to deal with peaks in the number of applicants.

The provision approach will have higher value for control and accountability added as it is somewhat simpler to assign responsibility to the unit producing the output; however, the approach will only connect to the perceived value of the output. The number of teaching hours is not useful for planning unless consumption of this provision by pupils is considered.

In sum, planning requires, or at least can benefit from, some focus on the likely consumption of goods and services. Government should not be in the business of producing goods and services that are unwanted or unusable. However, since in the real world there are many intervening variables between the anticipated demand and the actual consumption, broadly speaking, agencies or individuals can best be held accountable for the provision of services.

This produces a suggested relationship between the design and use of output measures as set out in Table 3.5.

Table 3.5 **Relationship between the basis of output measures and their use**

		Type of decision-making	
		A. Planning	**B. Accountability and control**
Basis of output measures[1]	1. Transaction (consumption)	A1. Consumption informs planning Possible use – when combined with demographic data	B1. Consumption determines targets and consequences Difficult use – hard to attribute responsibility
	2. Provision	A2. Provision informs planning Weak use – no check on the relevance of the goods and services produced	B2. Provision determines targets and consequences Possible use – but partial unless combined with some evaluation of the effectiveness of the output

Notes:

1. For easy and hard to measure, and individual and collective services.

3.2.4. Responding to complexity

As noted above, the intrinsic measurability of different outputs varies, and this is related to the distinction between individual and collective services.

The New Zealand output classes approach has, in effect, produced a single spectrum that starts with goods and services with a strong emphasis on a customer focus (individual goods, relatively easy to measure). The scale moves through two succeeding groups (transactions and professional/ managerial) which retain strong customer elements but which also exhibit professional or other criteria which might not be evident to the customer (individual goods, harder to measure). Two of the next three groups (investigations and control) involve government outputs with strong coercive elements and hence the task is a mixture of outputs focused on the individual and on the broader public (mixture of individual and collective goods, easy and hard to measure). Behavioural outputs are placed here in the spectrum and reflect outputs that, although individual, are distinctively hard to measure. The final group (*e.g.* contingent military capabilities) covers fully collective goods with no individual customer and are particularly hard to measure as they entail maintenance of a capability that will only be tested in the event of an emergency. Examples of transaction and provision approaches can be found within each class.

Table 3.6 New Zealand output classes

Output class groups	Description
1. Customer-oriented	These outputs have identifiable individual customers who voluntarily consume a service for their benefit. The key measure of quality is meeting customer expectations, usually assessed by way of an independent robust survey. Typically, a survey will emphasise customer requirements, such as relevance, response time, and helpfulness. The customer's view is paramount for determining quality for these outputs. An example in this group is lending library material.
2. Transactions	In contrast to Group 1, these output classes involve the large-scale processing of identical transactions, for example, assessment of unemployment benefit applications. Error rates, response times, average and marginal unit costs tend to be the most important characteristics of performance. Although individuals such as taxpayers or beneficiaries are affected by these transactions, they are not customers who either pay for or who can choose to use the service. Examples in this group include benefit payments and tax return processing.
3. Professional/ managerial	These output classes are characterised by a mixture of ongoing service and projects. Quantities are often variable and priority is placed on qualitative assessments against agreed criteria. This structured judgment approach may involve a recipient assessing against the criteria, but also require other professional input to assist in establishing proof of quality, for example in science research. Often these are core services directly used by ministers. The most significant output class in this group is policy advice.

Table 3.6 New Zealand output classes (continued)

Output class groups	Description
4. Investigations	These are public good outputs where considerations of risk, due process, legal compliance and quality of judgement are most important. The ability of the purchaser to judge their agents is often problematic. Citizens, as offenders or victims, rather than the purchasing minister, experience how these services are delivered. To what extent should the purchaser rely on trust in specifically selected officers, and how can the purchaser distinguish success from failure? The variability in the scale and type of investigations needs to be taken into account when specifying any quantities and unit costs. Criminal investigations are an example in this group.
5. Behavioural	These involve the purchaser contracting with a department to try to change individual attitudes and behaviours. Changes to awareness and behaviour of the individuals are of key importance in measurement. Performance measures relate to the success in achieving the desired level of individual or family change. Counselling is an example in this category.
6. Control	These outputs either involve the use of coercive powers to keep certain individuals within a controlled environment and prevent their escape, or prevent entry of individuals to a site or area. Performance measures relate to the success in achieving the desired level of control. An example in this group is prison management.
7. Emergency capabilities	These outputs involve the purchase of a planned level of response to emergencies based on average historical levels. The purchaser is concerned that a sufficient capability exists to meet various predetermined levels of risk so that an adequate response will be available in time to minimise loss, damage or injury. The purchaser wishes to know what the probability of success will be in dealing with the event. The performance measures need to provide assurance to the purchaser against these requirements.
8. Contingent military capabilities	These outputs involve the purchase of a minimum level of military capability, maintained to provide the government with options to respond to threats to New Zealand's national sovereignty or interests. Within the appropriation, the operational forces of the New Zealand Defence Force (NZDF) are maintained, and undertake prescribed levels of readiness training to assure the government that, within their specified degrees of notice, they could be activated and deploy to contribute to peace support, regional or collective security operations. The performance measures need to provide assurance that the operational forces of the NZDF could prepare and operate effectively in a plausible range of circumstances within representative degrees of notice.

Source: Based on *www.treasury.govt.nz/publicsector/pag/commonalities.asp,* accessed May 2006.

Although the New Zealand structure of output classes is undoubtedly a useful and time-saving device, strictly the allocation of particular outputs to these categories has a degree of arbitrariness. For example, health service outputs might be regarded as customer-oriented (class 1). However, it could equally be regarded as class 7, in the sense that it is important that the facility exists even when it is not needed.

3.3. Adding it up

Summarising the situation, Table 3.7 sets out the tradeoffs involved in determining the basis and use of output measures in planning and accountability/control decisions.

Table 3.7 Tradeoffs between the basis and use of output measures

Type of decision-making	
A. Planning	**B. Accountability and control**
Technically and politically difficult to make a tight connection between output measures and planning – and tight connections create stronger incentives for gaming. Loose connection more plausible, but the impact of output measures can be diluted. Transaction (consumption) approach is more promising as the basis for output measures used for planning.	Tight connection with output measures produces a strong enforcement effect – but this can be undermined by the incentives that this provides for gaming. When used more loosely as the basis for discussions, output measures have a weaker enforcement effect – but gaming can be mitigated. Provision approach is more promising as the basis for output measures used for accountability and control, but this begs the question as to the effectiveness of the output.

Notes

1. Most recently, the OECD Working Party of Senior Budget Officials meeting on "Experiences in Utilising Performance Information in Budget and Management Processes" held in Paris on 2-3 May 2006.

2. In the terms of Wilson (1989), functions can be production or procedural (in which the actions of the staff can be observed but the outputs are observable or not, respectively), "craft" (in which outcomes can be observed but not the outputs such as many police or social work tasks) or "coping" (in which neither outcomes or outputs can be observed, such as the diplomatic service). Kuhry *et al.* (2005) makes a similar distinction between service delivery, supervising activities and policy development (*uitvoering, aansturing* en *beleidsontwikkeling*) in their review of the performance of municipalities. Measurement tends to be easy in the first case, not in the least because there are usually consumers or consumption activities which can be counted. Supervising activities (*e.g.* of a Ministry of Education or municipalities with respect to schools) can be assigned as overhead to the supervised activities. In the case of policy development, measurement is particularly difficult.

3. Note that time periods overlap.

    This movement in the United Kingdom is somewhat counter to Graham Scott's observation that: "The experience of GPRA (Government Performance and Results Act) in the United States shows, in my view, that the attempt to commit an entire government to outcome-based performance accountability is problematical. The practicality of implementation forces the use of proxies for outcomes and measures of government activity that result in a situation that is very close to an output-oriented system that is augmented by measures and indicators of performance. A decade of experience across countries at the leading edge of public management leads me to conclude that outputs are superior to outcomes as the tool for linking the management plans of public organisations to the processes of budgeting and financial accountability, both between the executive and the parliament, and within the executive" (Scott, 2001, 200-201).

4. Planning can be around the nature of the outputs to be provided, the processes to be followed, or around how capacity is to be built.

5.   The functions of the budget are: *i)* to maintain aggregate fiscal discipline; *ii)* to allocate resources in accord with government priorities; and *iii)* to promote the efficient delivery of services; and *iv)* to provide authorisation for spending. This classification collapses the first three under the broad heading of planning, and the fourth under accountability and control.

In principle, output measures are also used in relationships between individuals and government, and sub-national and national governments. These relationships may entail legally binding contracts with the government in which commitments on either side are defined in terms of outputs. Sutherland *et al.* (2005) point out that gaming can be an issue if output measures are used for decision-making in intergovernmental relationships.

6.   Bird *et al.* (2005) point out that such indicators have created a new form of political accountability. Although indicators for the public services have "typically been designed to assess the impact of government policies on those services, or to identify well-performing or under-performing institutions and public servants", they have an additional role "the public accountability of Ministers for their stewardship of the public services" (Bird *et al.*, 2005).

7.   This mirrors the situation between a private sector supplier and customer. The trigger for turning away from a given supplier is the breakdown of trust, not some specific failing on an output agreement.

Chapter 4. Outcome Measurement: Key Issues

4.1. Introduction

Outcomes are those events, occurrences, or conditions that are the intended or unintended results of government actions. They happen "out there", in society, rather than "in here" inside public organisations. They concern what the graduate can do and understand rather than what lessons and support s/he has received at university; whether the pensioner can live a normal life on the state pension rather than whether it was paid correctly and on time; whether biodiversity is actually preserved rather than whether the environmental inspectorate carried out the required number of inspections according to plan. Thus, outcomes are generally of direct importance to service users and the general public. For example, in a social policy programme to improve financial management of families, outputs (what the service produces) are the number of counselling sessions or the number of families able to participate in financial management training. However, the desired outcomes include improvements (absolute or relative) in families' financial status, *e.g.* having more families living within a budget.

In distinction to outputs, outcomes often cannot be simply attributed to government actions or processes – other factors (often outside of government's control) are frequently involved.[1] This has implications for the use of outcome measures in relation to accountability and operational control. Commonly one cannot hold particular organisations – or even governments – fully responsible for outcomes in the same way that one can hold them responsible for outputs. On the other hand, they are not entirely without responsibility either: very frequently they make a contribution to the final outcome but cannot wholly determine it. Thus, for example, health care services definitely make a contribution to the health status of the community (particularly with respect to certain treatable conditions) but cannot determine that final status because of other factors such as diet, exercise and environmental hazards. Therefore, our treatment of outcomes needs to be subtle and nuanced.

The potential of outcome measurement varies with the particular service or sector. In some, outcomes cannot be sensibly measured until the programmes/policies have been running for many years (*e.g.* early childhood education for the socially disadvantaged or programmes to combat global warming). In others, however, outcomes can be measured more swiftly and surely, and can therefore be used more directly to assess the programme provided (*e.g.* a programme to reduce car crime in a specific location, a health education programme to raise awareness of the need for safe sex).If the purpose of public policy action is to contribute towards the achievement of specified outcome targets, then it is reasonable to ask whether those outcomes were subsequently achieved. However, assessing performance against outcome targets can usually be done only generally. In considering, for example, the UK Foreign and Commonwealth Office outcome targets which included "a reduction in the number of people whose lives are affected by violent conflict and a reduction in potential sources of future conflict, where the United Kingdom can make a significant contribution" (H.M. Treasury, 2001) then the problem of attribution becomes clear.

4.2. What outcome measures do governments use?

Many and diverse public sector outcome measures are used at the programme, agency or sector level. Collectively, these are of tremendous importance, but, for obvious reasons, they cannot all be spelled out here. They include such diverse indicators as infant mortality, level of adult illiteracy, recorded crime, the ratio between wages for men and for women, and the percentage of the population below the official poverty line. Historically, and still today, the desire of public service professionals to improve these "conditions" is a powerful force for social improvement. What is more, comparative studies can be a significant influence on domestic debates – when the citizens of country X are told that their infant mortality rate is higher than country Y, and country Y has a lower GNP per capita than X, it provides reformers with potent information to argue for improvement.

In addition to such specific measures there are also more general measures or indices. At the societal or whole-of-government level, such outcome measures are increasingly described as "well-being" measures. As Summers and Heston (1999) note "[t]he concept [of] well-being … has a number of dimensions [including m]aterial well-being flowing from the availability of goods and services, expressed in either current or long-run terms, and [n]on-material well-being, for example, longevity, defined for the kinds of welfare conditions that do not necessarily flow simply from the availability of goods and services". Well-being measures are perhaps best exemplified by the datasets in the various national "Suites of Indicators".[2] Some of the better known are Measures of Australia's Progress (MAP) which has just released its 4th publication; the UK's Quality of Life Counts (first published in 1999); Switzerland's development of Quality of Life indicators; Measuring Ireland's Progress (published in 2003 and 2005); Canada's Performance and the United States' Key National Indicators Initiative which is moving toward becoming a web-based database allowing users to combine variables to measure progress according to their priorities and on a local level (Matthews, 2006).

These "suites" include key education, health, environment, economic and other indicators covering, for example, educational attainment, life expectancy at birth, air quality, etc.

Box 4.1 An increasing focus on capital within well-being indicators

The Australian Bureau of Statistics is moving towards a "capital" approach as the underpinning framework in its data collection and presentation. A possible approach is under development and will allow sustainability to be assessed as well as progress.

In its year 2000 budget, the government of Canada asked the National Roundtable on the Environment and the Economy to develop recommendations for a small set of environmentally sustainable development indicators. A wide range of discussions and consultations led to the adoption of a "capital approach" with the recommendation for a small set of easily understood indicators that would be produced and published annually by Statistics Canada. These indicators cover: air quality, water quality, greenhouse gas emissions, forest cover, extent of wetlands and educational attainment.

In March 2006, Statistics Finland published a statistical review on social capital in Finland. Following largely the OECD definition of social capital, the report contains materials from existing statistical sources. It does not aim to provide any indicators of social capital, simply because there is no common international understanding on the dimensions such indicators should cover. Neither does the report aim at an analysis of the link between social capital and well-being, although such a link has been suggested both in international and national research and in policy debate. The discussion on the role of social capital and well-being in Finland has mainly concerned the assumed positive health effects of social capital.

Box 4.1 An increasing focus on capital within well-being indicators (continued)

Statistics Netherlands considers that knowledge is closely linked to the measurement of well-being as it affects the future of a society in its core. Sustainability of an economy is highly dependent on the knowledge within a society and so productivity statistics and productivity accounts will be a priority. These productivity accounts will not be limited to labour productivity only but will also include capital.

In the United Kingdom, work was supposed to commence in the autumn of 2006 to develop a set of well-being measures, with the view to publication in 2007. This was likely to draw on existing statistical work from across government in areas such as social capital and mental health. Another survey was also commissioned which would include questions on life satisfaction.

Notes: See OECD (2001c) for a discussion of social capital in particular.

Source: Matthews (2006).

Annex 3 sets out the well-being measures that are most often included in the "suites". Box 4.2 suggests some criteria that appear to explain the selection of measures employed.

Box 4.2 Apparent criteria for well-being indicators

A review of the well-being measures used by countries (see Annex 2) suggests that they are, *de facto*, selected on the criteria that they are:

1.   generally desired by citizens;

2.   probably significantly affected by government actions;

3.   not easily attributable to the outputs from a single sector (although they can be, and often are, readily attributable to the activities of government as a whole);

4.   entailing measures that are available at reasonable cost.

As will be discussed below, it is not proposed to encompass such broad measures of outcome in any public management data collection effort. Instead, it is proposed to explore the possibility of developing some narrower measures which reflect, to some significant degree, activities of the executive arm of government.

4.3. Origins and growth of well-being measures

To some extent, well-being measures have been developed as a reaction to the limitations of Gross Domestic Product (GDP) as a measure of societal progress. The key concern with GDP as a measure of progress is that it fails to identify improvements in, or harm to, social structures or the environment, sustainability of growth, non-market household activities such as unpaid child-care, quality of life issues such as the availability of leisure time, or the distribution of national income.[3]

In a way, this critique is unfair to the initiators of the SNA. The SNA initially had no intention of measuring societal progress. Simon Kuznets, a founding father of the SNA, warned the U.S. Congress in the 1940s: "The welfare of a nation can scarcely be inferred from a measurement of national income as defined (by the GDP) … Goals for more growth should specify of what and for what" (quoted in Anielski, 2002). Although GDP was not designed as a measure of societal performance, it was almost immediately interpreted as such. In the absence of good comparative statistics on social progress and quality of life, GDP quickly became the yardstick for social progress.

Matthews (2006) notes that the early 1970s saw the "social indicators movement" create considerable academic and social policy attention concerning the construction and use of key measures of societal progress. Amongst others, this lead to the creation, in 1970, of the "OECD Programme of Work and Social Indicators" as a result of concerns about the limitations of economic measures of progress. OECD (1982) provided 33 indicators together with accompanying statistical specifications and guidelines for data collection, for member countries to measure their social progress. Besides international institutions, many governments took initiatives during the 1970s; examples include Austria, Belgium, Denmark, France, Germany, the Netherlands, Norway, Sweden and the United Kingdom (Noll, 1996).

In the next decade, however, the social indicator movement stagnated. In particular in the United States and in some international institutions, initiatives were scaled back (Van Dooren and Aristigueta, 2005). The reasons for this evolution have been extensively studied. Cobb and Rixfors (1998) summarise the seven main factors:

- economic anxieties which pushed aside concerns about social issues;

- the ideological shift toward conservatism and distrust of government (and a decrease of government support for social indicator research);

- the limited usefulness of social indicators to policy makers;

- the lack of a theoretical framework comparable to economic theory;

- the lack of an agreed-upon method of making normative judgments (about whether trends are good or bad);

- the lack of a common unit of measurement to permit aggregation, comparable to the use of money in economics;

- the declining faith in econometric modelling, which failed to avert rising inflation and unemployment.

By the end of the 1990s, a new interest in well-being measures could be identified. In addition to the social indicator movement, there was by then a stronger emphasis on sustainable development and environmental indicators. The publication of the handbook *Satellite System for Integrated Environmental and Economic Accounts* in 2003 is an example of this trend. This was an extension of the 1993 version of the System of National Accounts, and was jointly published by the United Nations, OECD, International Monetary Fund, European Commission and the World Bank. It gives an overview of various ways to put into practice the definition of sustainable development proposed by the Brundtland Commission. Another example is the development of Material Flows Accounting which tracks the amounts of materials – as classes or individual substances – that enter the economy, accumulate in capital stock such as housing or automobiles, or exit to the environment as waste. Material flows indicators have been adopted in a growing number of countries and are now regularly published by the EU and some member countries. A final example is the compilation of "sustainable development indicators for the European Union" from Eurostat, which sets out 110 indicators addressing: climate change and clean energy; threats to public health; management of natural resources; transport and land use; poverty and social exclusion; and the economic and social implications of an ageing society (Eurostat, 2005).

The renewed interest in well-being measures was not limited to sustainable development. Other initiatives still included the traditional social indicators. In 2002, the OECD launched Society at a Glance. This publication is a biannual compendium of social indicators intended to shed light on two issues: "how far OECD countries have progressed in terms of social development; and to what extent this progress has been the result of deliberate policy actions, either by government or institutions" (OECD, 2005d). Indicators are grouped into five main categories: background indicators to provide the overall context in which social policy operates, and four categories that reflect the main objectives of social policy – self-sufficiency, equity, health, and social cohesion.

Other developments that could contribute to more comprehensive measures of well-being and progress have included:

- The development of social accounting matrices also based upon the national accounts which link the mainly macro-statistics of national accounts with the mainly micro-statistics of labour markets and households. One of the most advanced uses of this tool is the Dutch System of Economic and Social Accounting Matrices and Extensions which links economic, social and environmental data in one unified system of accounts measured in various units.

- On a similar "suite" approach, the OECD Factbook provides a global overview of world economic, social and environmental trends, bringing together 100 indicators for evaluating the relative position of any OECD member country concerning: population and migration, macroeconomic trends, economic globalisation, prices, labour market, science and technology, environment, education, public policies, quality of life and globalisation.

- The Human Development Index (HDI) was proposed in 1990 by the United Nations Development Programme (UNDP) as a composite indicator to assess the three main dimensions of development: longevity, knowledge, and the standard of living. Longevity is measured by life expectancy at birth; knowledge is measured by adult literacy rate combined with gross enrolment ratio for primary, secondary, and tertiary schools; and standard of living is measured by GDP per capita in purchasing power parity US dollars. HDI is the unweighted average of the three (UNDP, 2005).

- The Index of Economic Well-being, developed by the Centre for the Study of Living Standards in 1998, comprises four components of economic well-being: consumption flows, wealth stocks, income distribution and economic security.

4.4. Measures can provide a frame or vision for subsequent policy decisions

One significant use of outcome measures is to provide a frame in which policy debates can take place. This section elaborates that potential.

Outcome measures can be used as inspiration or, more cynically, rationalisation for a broad set of policy initiatives. This focus on outcomes arguably creates "a 'mental model' for awareness, understanding, and thinking prior to choosing" (Riche, 2003).

By providing a target on the horizon, outcome measures are intended to achieve two key results. First, they are intended to focus policy thinking – providing a framework or an orientation within which other planning and accountability decisions will be made. Second, it is intended to inspire extended organisational and individual effort.

The first use has two aspects. Outcome measures such as the European Structural Indicators create a mental "frame" – "pre-digested reasoning that creates an interpretation for facts" (De Biase, 2005). Such mental frames can lead to voluntary policy alignment. "The use of structural indicators is an example of this new way to design common policies at the European level and to promote convergence among member states through, among others, a common definition of objectives and a common set of indicators to monitor the progress and the convergence" (Munoz, 2005).

Box 4.3 Outcomes as a broad focus for policy thinking

Canadian government departments use a broad framework of strategic outcomes to measure their performance. The following is one example.

Analysis of performance by strategic outcome: Good governance and effective institutions for First Nations, Inuit and Northerners, built on co-operative relationships

Indian and Northern Affairs Canada (INAC) and Canadian Polar Commission

This strategic outcome encompasses helping First Nations and Inuit communities to develop effective governance and institutions that support achieving an improved quality of life. First Nations governments and Inuit communities are increasingly responsible for their own affairs as evidenced by devolution, self-government agreements, and new intergovernmental and treaty relationships. These developments support First Nation and Inuit communities' efforts to develop clear accountability to citizens, and to help improve community social and economic conditions. INAC's continued support of good governance and effective institutions assists First Nation and Inuit communities to benefit from economic development. At the same time, federal, provincial and territorial governments are building foundations for co-operative relationships with First Nation and Inuit communities.

Progress on the Aboriginal agenda and on northern institution-building contributes to the beginning of a social and cultural revitalization in northern communities and to strengthened partnerships essential to current and future economic development. Further attention to these priorities and to supporting the capacity of territorial governments to deliver programs and services within their jurisdiction is essential. Strong northern governance also has an important role in addressing circumpolar issues.

Source : www.tbs-sct.gc.ca/rma/dpr1/04-05/INAC-AINC/INAC-AINCd4503_e.asp

---

By creating such "frames", outcomes are particularly useful for public and political policy debate. Ultimately they reflect the issues that engage popular concern, and sidestep the more technical questions about processes and outputs. Politicians think and work in terms of outcomes and the purpose of government policies is often phrased in terms of outcomes.

This use of outcome measures to focus a debate also has particular significance in the case of complex outcome objectives which involve contributions of diverse sectors and agencies within government (Kristensen *et al.*, 2001). In those circumstances, the outcome measure is intended to act as a high-level disciplining device to encourage a collaborative discussion on the relevant contributions of each actor involved. Lonti and Gregory (2007) describe the effect of the New Zealand Public Finance Amendment Act 2004 which came into force in January 2005. By allowing more flexibility in the use of resources, within a tightened requirement that appropriations specify the outcomes that government actions are to achieve or contribute towards, the act is intended to counter the "silo effect". Parliamentary appropriations do not now have to be confined to one output class and the legislation allows a department effectively to transfer its appropriation for outputs to another department.

The government of Canada "whole-of-government framework" has a similar purpose. It is structured around three key policy areas (sustainable economy, social foundations and Canada's place in the world). Each policy area is subdivided into "Government of Canada Outcomes", which are the "long-term and enduring benefits to Canadians that federal departments, agencies and Crown corporations are working to achieve".[4] Each outcome is then associated with departmental and agency level outcomes and Crown corporation mandates (see Box 4.3). Bellefeuille-Prégent and Wilson (2005) note that the Canadian Treasury Board Secretariat is considering the development of a whole-of-government planning report that could make the link between societal indicator reporting and government-wide planning more explicit. Similarly, the state level suite of indicators prepared by the State of Victoria, Australia – Growing Victoria Together – had as one of its primary aims to encourage government departments to work better together when tackling cross-cutting issues of concern (Hall *et al.*, 2005).

Outcome indicators have a role not just in focusing political debate, but in broadening the involvement of the wider public in policy making. Those who develop outcome indicators for this purpose argue that advancements in Information and Communication Technologies (ICT) have changed the way in which markets and societies work, with the Internet in particular making information more accessible to citizens than before. They suggest that the ideal of the "fully informed decision maker" could be a reality. But if that reality is to be achieved, the information must become knowledge. Sets of outcome indicators are seen as one way to provide a wide audience with a digestible set of information with which they can understand the performance of their country, or government. This information can encourage them to better influence policy makers and help them make more informed decisions when holding policy makers accountable (Giovannini and Uyshal, 2006).

The second framing purpose of outcome indicators is to direct managerial and individual attention towards a set of higher-level goals or purposes that few would disagree with and that might inspire additional effort (see Box 4.4 and Hatry, 2004; Hatry *et al.*, 2003; Perrin, 2006).

Box 4.4 Enthusiasts note that outcome measurement offers performance dividends

"This (outcome measurement) dividend doesn't take years to occur. It often starts appearing early in the process of setting up an outcome measurement system. Just the process of focusing on outcomes – on why the program[me] is doing what it's doing and how it thinks participants will be better off – gives program[me] managers and staff a clearer picture of the purpose of their efforts. That clarification alone frequently leads to more focused and productive service delivery ... It can, for example, help program[me]s:

1. recruit and retain talented staff;

2. enlist and motivate able volunteers;

3. attract new participants;

4. engage collaborators;

5. garner support for innovative efforts;

6. win designation as a model or demonstration site;

7. retain or increase funding;

8. gain favourable public recognition."

Source : United Way (2006).

Tallis (2005) considers that this framing purpose is where outcome measures can contribute most readily. He notes that, in principle, outcome measures can contribute towards:

- Policy focus – drawing attention to aspects of society that merit attention or intervention.

- Policy design – developing a detailed strategy for a social intervention or for encouraging an environment in which social improvement can occur.

- Policy evaluation – assessing the effectiveness of interventions in achieving desired social outcomes.

He concludes that their strength is in contributing to a sharpened policy focus.

4.5. Filling an apparent gap

One dimension where it has been suggested that new outcome indicators are desirable is that of "governance". Box 4.5 gives some indication of recent developments. However, it should be noted that "governance" is a somewhat vague concept and – in most but not all of its definitions – is more to do with processes and outputs rather than genuine outcomes. Nevertheless, we include this information as a base point from which further discussions of possible outcome measures may take off.

Reducing the vast and somewhat formless territory of governance down to "executive governance" might offer more hope.[5] Part of the problem is that broad measures of governance such as transparency or rule of law implicate all parts of the state – including electoral institutions and the legislature, and the functioning of the judiciary. It might be possible to identify a set of outcomes that meet the same apparent criteria as other existing "well-being" measures (Box 4.1), but which reflect institutional arrangements (not policy objectives) within the executive (not the legislature or judiciary).

Box 4.5 Governance indicators

Over the last 30 years, there has been a significant increase in the number and range of indicators, purporting to measure a rather broad notion of governance.[1] The theoretical basis behind the indicators is uncertain. Public management as a field of study and practitioner debate is fraught with definitional problems, but there is some general consensus as to what is included. Few would take issue with the proposition that: "public management reforms consist of deliberate changes to the structures and processes of public sector organisations with the objective of getting them (in some sense) to run better" (Pollitt and Bouckaert, 2004). In essence, public management focuses on the plumbing of the public sector – how money is used, how people are motivated and how organisations are structured.

By contrast, the parameters of governance are less clear. "… [W]hile empirical research links governance-related institutions and development, there is not yet a consensus as to how to approach governance and its measurement" (International Monetary Fund and World Bank, 2006). The idea of governance is undoubtedly identifying a real and pressing issue – and all practitioners with experience of developing or post-conflict countries would accept that the roots of problems concerning corruption or major service delivery failures are not be found within the public sector management plumbing. Broader political economy issues, such as capture of the state apparatus by entrenched interests, deliberate opacity in political party financing and corrupt judiciary, are both the consequences and the causes of the performance failures. However, exactly what is within this concept and, equally significantly, what and how any elements of it can be changed is far from clear.

The absence of a well-accepted theoretical framework for governance ensures that any composite indicators are largely devices for communication – for crystallising concerns about corruption, etc. into a single short and pithy summary. This is undoubtedly a useful contribution to structuring the dialogue between donor agencies and developing countries –particularly when accompanied by more explicitly qualitative assessments (Doig *et al.*, 2006). However, where the concerns about broader notions of governance are less pressing, where egregious corruption and massive service delivery failure are relatively rare, then the value of the indicators is somewhat limited for two reasons.

First, the accuracy of the indicators is often insufficient for a more nuanced policy debate. Individual governance indicators tend to be perception-based, which can be problematic unless triangulated with some more fact-based indicators. Composite indicators generally combine the problems inherent in an over-reliance on perception-based data, with additional difficulties resulting from the aggregation process. Without a clear theoretical framework, it is not clear what the indicator is attempting to measure other than in a general and intuitive sense (Besançon, 2003).

> ### Box 4.5 Governance indicators (continued)
>
> Second, and as a consequence of the over-reliance on perception-based indicators, and the resort to intricate aggregation methodologies, the resulting indicators provide very little policy guidance. Arguably, they indicate that a particular institutional area within a particular country is indeed in poor (or good) shape – however, they offer little or no insights into the steps that should be taken to improve the situation.[2]
>
> *Notes:*
>
> 1. These are primarily intended for the use of, or at least for promulgation by, development agencies. The initial crop of governance indicators emerged during the early 1990s, coinciding with the rediscovery that governance matters for development. This was perhaps a useful corrective to the technocratic emphasis of much of the development debate of the time. The growth in the number and coverage of indicators was substantial. Considering only the 14 sources of expert- and survey-based indicators used by Kaufmann *et al.* in their first aggregation exercise (Kaufmann *et al.*: 1999), the vast majority of them did not exist before 1995. With the exception of the Freedom House political and civil liberties indicators, those that did exist were intended solely to evaluate "political risks" faced by foreign investors, and development researchers and practitioners were unaware of and/or uninterested in them until the 1990s. It was in 1998, roughly, the year when it was unambiguously accepted that institutions matter (World Bank, 1997) – and the array of indicators has continued to grow since that time. See Knack and Manning (2000). Arndt and Oman (2006) and the Governance Data Web-interactive Inventory of Datasets and Empirical Tools (2006) provide useful overviews of recent work in constructing broad measures of "governance". The Governance Data Web-interactive Inventory of Datasets and Empirical Tools (2006) lists 139 governance indicators.
>
> 2. See Knack *et al.* (2003) for a more detailed discussion of this point.

Measuring Australia's Progress offers some examples of possible outcome measures along these lines (Australian Bureau of Statistics, 2006). Box 4.6 sets out the development goals for state services in New Zealand. They comprise a perhaps not unfamiliar mixture. Some are genuine outcomes, but others are not. Thus "trust in the state services" is an outcome, but "trustworthiness exhibited by state servants" (a rather difficult concept to operationalise) is an output rather than an outcome. Other elements in the goal structure are processes, such as "the extent to which a learning and development framework is used".

Box 4.6 Development goals for state services in New Zealand

In March 2005 the government of New Zealand agreed an ambitious set of Development Goals for the State Services. The 2006 progress report notes that the ideas behind these goals are not new, but, by making them clear and visible, and by setting timelines for progress, starting with milestones for 2007 and 2010, a clear agenda has been set for the State Services (New Zealand State Services Commission, 2006) although of course the problem of obtaining supporting hard data remains.

Development goal	Indicator
Employer of choice	
Ensure the State Services is an employer of choice attractive to high achievers with a commitment to service	1 Reputation: Perceptions of the State Services as a place to work 2 Staff engagement: Engagement levels of staff in State Services agencies
Excellent state servants	
Develop a strong culture of constant learning in pursuit of excellence	Staff: 1 State servants' perceptions about the effectiveness of development plans, processes and opportunities Chief executive/agency: 2 The extent to which agencies are specifying the competencies they require of their people to meet current and future organisational needs Sector: 3 The extent to which a learning and development framework is used across the sector to improve agencies' performance.
Networked State Services	
Use technology to transform the provision of services for New Zealanders	1 Grouping of services/transactions that apply technology to allow an individual – from one place at the same time – to access multiple programmes 2 Channel synchronisation of government transactions – within an agency or across government 3 The extent to which technology supports a user having to give the same information to government only once
Co-ordinated state agencies	
Ensure the total contribution of government agencies is greater than the sum of its parts	1 The extent to which behaviours exhibited by state servants support co-ordination in pursuit of results 2 The extent to which systems support strategy, design and service delivery staff to work together
Accessible State Services	
Enhance access, responsiveness and effectiveness, and improve New Zealanders' experience of State Services	Accessible State Services: 1 Target group uptake of services Responsive State Services: 2 Appropriateness of referral Effective State Services: 3 Users' experience and expectations inform service design and improvement
Trusted State Services	
Strengthen trust in the State Services, and reinforce the spirit of service	1 Trustworthiness exhibited by state servants 2 The extent of New Zealanders' confidence in the integrity of state servants when delivering services
Source : New Zealand State Services Commission (2006).	

We are left with the tricky question of what outcomes might be serviceable as indicators of the performance of executive government. Box 4.7 offers some preliminary guidance in this matter.

Box 4.7 Selecting executive governance outcomes

The literature concerning the outcomes that might be more distinctly attributable to institutional arrangements within the executive (executive governance outcomes) than to other contributors to governance (electoral institutions and the legislature, the judiciary, free media, etc.) suggests that they fall into at least three broad and overlapping categories: equity, fiscal/economic stability and public confidence. Arguably, environmental sustainability offers a fourth "executive governance outcome" – although this is probably more closely related to policy objectives than to institutional arrangements.

Michalos (2006) sets out the key dimensions of equity in service provision, and social outcomes. This is clearly a key concern for OECD member country governments and relates to a traditional value of the public sector: impartiality. Many commentators have associated this with representativeness within the public sector on the basis that impartiality is all but impossible in practice without this.[1]

Fiscal and economic stability in the sense of avoiding, or at least managing, shocks and in ensuring inter-generational equity are well-recognised as goals. Providing greater fiscal room for manoeuvre through reducing budgetary deficits is often identified as a concern (Schick, 2003, for example). Inter-generational inequity is most often discussed in terms of state pension arrangements which provide extensive benefits but which may defer costs to future generations of tax-payers (see OECD, 2005e). It should of course be kept in mind that fiscal discipline is certainly not simply attributable to isolated policy or institutional reforms within the executive. Hallerberg (2004) points out that some member states with the ideal institutional arrangements for fiscal discipline are still incurring deficits in violation of the Maastricht Treaty's excessive deficit procedure and the Stability and Growth Pact because of political pressures and electoral and party systems.

Overarching these two key categories of "executive governance outcomes", public confidence in the public sector is a key concern, and closely relates to the perceived legitimacy of government and the willingness to pay taxes (Bird, 2004; OECD, 2005c).

Box 4.7 Selecting executive governance outcomes (continued)

The empirical aspects of many measures of trust are hard to unravel largely because of the conceptual problems about what is being trusted (OECD, 2000). However, it seems increasingly the case that confidence can be improved through demonstrated responsiveness on the part of the public service to political priorities. Responsiveness to political priorities is now widely seen as a legitimate way of being responsible to the citizens (Dunn, 1997; Hood and Peters, 2004; Self, 1972). At a time of increasingly frequent public-opinion polls, e-mail, call-in radio and television surveys, greater responsiveness is expected of the administration (Rosenthal, 1997). As Schick (2005) has pointed out, governments must increasingly earn their legitimacy through delivering on their service delivery promises. Moreover, governments are also expected to lead and to inform public opinion, not just by following it to get short-term votes.

Notes:
1. An early exploration of the relationship between impartiality and representativeness was provided by Kaufman (1956). Others have picked up the baton and debated the risks and benefits of active representation and generally agree with Mosher (1968) in coming down on the side of passive representation – i.e. the belief that if the rules are fair and balanced, then selecting merit will (more or less) automatically lead to representativeness.

4.6. Developing comparative measures concerning trust in government

Gaining (regaining, some would argue) the trust of citizens has emerged as a core concern for governments.[6] Babb (2005) identifies trust in government as an aspect of social capital along with civic participation, membership of social networks, and social participation through involvement in groups and voluntary activities.

4.6.1. Could trust measures be equivalent to other well-being measures?

Can some measure of trust meet the criteria for well-being indicators set out in Box 4.2?

Is it generally desired by citizens? It is hard to imagine a preference for living in a country with an untrustworthy government or civil service any more than one can imagine a preference for particularly poor air quality or short life expectancy. Improving trust in government is certainly one of the common features of discussions concerning the need for various types of public sector reform, and so by popular conviction at the very least, it must be regarded as an outcome. There is certainly a technocratic consensus that it is desirable. Van de Walle *et al.* (2005) point out from their review of the literature that high levels of public trust stimulate public sector productivity, since trusting citizens are more willing to comply with regulations and procedures, lowering transaction costs. But there is more to it than this. Trusting citizens are also more likely to be willing to play their part in the "co-production" of many services, especially in the healthcare, education and social services sectors, but also elsewhere. This goes well beyond compliance and becomes active, constructive engagement in the planning, delivery and assessment of a wide range of public services. Having trusting citizens may also influence their willingness to make sacrifices during a crisis, to obey the law, to pay taxes or to serve in the military.

Is it significantly affected by government actions? This is both intuitively plausible and empirically supported. Chanley, Rudolph *et al.* (2000) try to show that, in the United States, negative perceptions of the economy, scandals associated with Congress, and increasing public concern about crime each lead to declining public trust in government. However, the connection is, to say the least, somewhat obscure. For example, Barnes and Gill (2000) and Bok (1997) found that confidence dropped while performance improved. It is probably significantly affected by government sector policy actions and outputs. For example, Breeman (2003) found evidence that trust was affected by government actions in the case of agriculture.

Is it not easily attributable to the outputs from a single sector? It is probably significantly affected by cross-cutting structures and systems within government. Yackee and Lowery (2005) for example, in the case of the United States federal bureaucracy, demonstrate that scandals or policy failures do have an impact on overall public approval ratings – and not just for the individual agency concerned (others are tarred with the same brush). Killerby (2005) shows, from World Values Survey Data, that confidence in the bureaucracy is not correlated with social trust or with life satisfaction, diminishing the argument that the public are taking out frustrations on government.[7]

Is it available at reasonable cost? There are already some key data relevant to trust offering some international comparability:

- World Values Study (WVS). This survey has been organised in four waves since 1981: 1981, 1990, 1995-1997 and 1999-2000. All OECD member countries have participated in one or more waves.

- Eurobarometer data provides data from survey questions concerning trust in the civil service, which was included several times since 1997, with the last measurement in Spring 2002.

- Many of the underlying data used in the construction of the World Bank Institute "Worldwide Governance Indicators" can be interpreted as measures of public and business trust in government (see *http://info.worldbank.org/governance/kkz2005/notes.html#kk*).

- The World Bank "Doing Business" database (see *www.doingbusiness.org*) provides a broad array of data concerning the regulatory costs of business, and can provide insights into business confidence in government.

However, there are many conceptual uncertainties in relation to the question that is being addressed in these surveys. On trust/confidence, survey questions would need to be framed which distinguish between the public's views of government policy and their views of the quality of the administration. It is the latter which is of institutional interest – but this would then need to be associated with some comparable units of analysis (which level of government, etc.), and some further distinction made between satisfaction concerning responses in the past, and trust in the quality of services in the future.

It seems at least feasible that the institutions already undertaking relevant surveys currently might be prepared to discuss collaboration within a larger effort.

4.6.2. Would such measures be policy relevant?

If it could be clarified, then the notion of trust in government as an institutional outcome could have distinct policy relevance. The proponents of particular institutional reforms suggest that there is an undoubted chain of connections from those institutional forms to improved trust:

- OECD work on ethics and conflict of interest argues that trust is enhanced by the reality of perceived integrity in public decision-making (OECD, 2000, 2003, 2005a). Others maintain that improved service delivery arrangements are key to improvements in trust (Cowell *et al.*, 2006; Heintzman and Marson, 2005; Humphreys, 2003; Kampen *et al.*, 2003; Van Ryzin *et al.*, 2004) – although this is challenged on both empirical and theoretical grounds by Bouckaert and Walle (2003) and Zouridis (2003).

- Heintzman and Marson (2005) have also suggested that citizen satisfaction is correlated with public service staff job satisfaction.

- OECD (2001) suggests that greater public participation is key to improved trust.

Others argue the reverse – with Suleiman (2005) concluding from an international comparative survey that more than two decades of unrelenting reforms of the state have produced no change (except for the worse) in voter turnout, confidence in politicians, and respect for public institutions. This raises a question of whether declines in some measures of trust are actually linked to "reform", or whether they happen independently. Others argue (Nevitte, 2006) that a reduction in trust might be a natural manifestation of a more robust democracy, with greater participation in less formal political activity.

Yet others have argued that the question is moot until there are better measures of service delivery and performance (Yang and Holzer, 2006).

4.6.3. Would measures of trust introduce a risk of gaming?

As a measure, trust does seem somewhat amenable to methodological cherry-picking as it is conceptually very elusive, with two dimensions of choice concerning measures. First, there is the question of what the phenomenon engenders in the citizen – is the citizen reporting that, in retrospect, s/he was satisfied with one or several services, or that s/he is prospectively trusting that future actions from government will be acceptable? Second, there is a set of very important questions concerning the unit of analysis – is the citizen referring to a particular service or entity or even politician, or to a major institutional area (e.g. civil service or Parliament), or to some abstract notion of government as a whole?

On the first dimension, Van de Walle *et al.* (2005) point out from their review of survey data that trust and satisfaction are frequently linked but far from identical. Negative overall views of government often coincide with quite positive evaluations of specific services.

On the second dimension concerning the unit of analysis, the World Values Study distinguishes between: the press, Parliament, labour unions, government, major companies, civil service, European Union, NATO, justice system, churches, social security system, United Nations, armed forces, health care system, police, education system, and political parties. However, the survey results indicate that different groups in the countries surveyed have very different views about these institutions. This may very plausibly mean that they have different experiences of these institutions – but it could also suggest that there is some uncertainty about what each of the institutional units represents. Van de Walle (2005) also notes that distrusting attitudes towards the civil service may coexist with very positive evaluations of some specific agencies, such as the fire department, the municipal administration or the postal system. They point out that this suggests that while actual experience with a service will dominate in a customer satisfaction survey, citizens are more likely to refer to their overall image of government or to stereotypical images of the bureaucracy when expressing an overall opinion of the public administration. Arguably, there is also a level of romanticisation concerning specific services that citizens rarely interact with. This might explain why certain types of services consistently receive higher scores than others. Fire departments are almost always evaluated much more positively than others, such as road repair services.

Van de Walle *et al.* (2005) reasonably, take the civil service to be the primary institutional unit when interpreting trust within the World Values Survey results. The National Election Studies use various measures of trust in government in the United States, but it is possible that the term government in the United States is interpreted more inclusively (traditionally the term refers to all three "branches" – executive, legislature and judiciary) and more politically (including elected officials) than in other countries.

The ambiguities in the way that trust can be measured could foster gaming if apparent declines in trust are "manufactured" at key moments in the political cycle. In particular, there is a frequent assertion that confidence in government (possibly interpreted as confidence in the civil service) has been in decline and it is the task of reformers or incoming governments to correct this trend through some radical reform programme (Nye *et al.*, 1997; Perry and Webster, 1999). "[T]he global reform movement is a symptom of – and a reaction to – the decline of public confidence in governmental institutions and performance" (Kettl, 2000). This persistent drumbeat of concern has been heard for over 30 years (Crozier *et al.*, 1975). Others note that measures of trust are sensitive over the short-term to the crises of the day and to media commentary (Barnes and Gill, 2000).

Bouckaert *et al.* (2005) find that decline in trust has been used to legitimize public sector reform. Similar points are made more passionately by Suleiman (2005) who argues that this has been a somewhat cynical approach by politicians who are keen to deflect criticism from their own inability to avoid inflation, deficits, and economic instability. Similar concerns have been expressed in relation to the United States by Garrett, Thurber *et al.* (2006).

In fact, the World Values Survey data do not reveal clear trends over time (Van de Walle *et al.*, 2005).

There are also country specific surveys which suggest diverse patterns:

- National Election Studies data in the United States do indeed show a decline in trust since the late 1950s. There has, however, been a significant recovery since 1994.

- In most European countries, recent trends can be mapped using Eurobarometer data. Trust in the civil service was included several times since 1997, with the last measurement in Spring 2002. Of the EU15 countries included in the 1997 and 2002 Eurobarometer surveys, only three faced a decline in trust (Van de Walle *et al.*, 2005).

4.7. Developing comparative measures concerning equity and economic and fiscal stability

Another function of outcome indicators may be as a check on the crucial social issue of equity. Are individual citizens in similar situations being treated equally? In principle it is possible to measure this in many areas, although actual existing measures are often less than complete. Such measures might reasonably cover the distribution of key services by socio-economic or other groups. Michalos (2006) provides a useful summary of possibilities.

Consideration could also be given to the development of outcome measures concerning fiscal/economic stability. Such measures might cover issues such as budgetary deficits (as a contributor to economic and fiscal instability) and other budgetary outcomes. There has already been extensive work examining the relationship between these outcomes and the institutional arrangements within government. Savage (2005) notes that OECD and other governments have attempted to restrain large-scale budgetary deficits and debt by institutional reforms which have created processes which are more centralised, "top-down" and "front-loaded" in order to reduce the influence of interest groups and budgetary claimants.[8] There have been extensive studies of the contribution of institutional arrangements to fiscal discipline.[9] Hallerberg (2004) has classified the key institutional drivers of these particular budgetary outcomes under three broad headings:

- "Delegation governance" entails centralised budgetary systems with strong finance ministries, with the ability to formulate budgets, monitor ministry behaviour, and enforce spending rules against spending ministries and free-spending ministries.

- "Commitment governance" refers to situations where "fiscal contracts" set a variety of spending, deficit, and other targets that require budgetary players to adhere to commitments.

- "Fiefdom governance" refers to situations where finance ministries are unable to control the demands of spending ministries and legislators for distributive project funding.

Notes

1.   This definition of outcomes is somewhat at odds with the narrower definition used, for example, in the US Government Performance and Results Act of 1993 (Sec. 2801 – Definitions) "For purposes of this chapter the term … 'outcome measure' refers to an assessment of the results of a program activity compared to its intended purpose".

A further distinction can be drawn between *intermediate* and *final* outcomes. Intermediate outcomes are a result of the public sector activities that are expected to lead to a desired end, but are not ends in themselves. Children attending classes represent an intermediate (and intrinsically valuable) outcome of the activity holding classes. However, the intended final outcome is more likely to be considered the degree to which the children gain competencies in core subjects. Intermediate outcomes can be more directly attributed to public sector activities than final outcomes and are reasonably included in the discussion of outputs.

Some governments draw a further distinction. The Canadian government looks at "immediate", "intermediate" and "final outcomes". Immediate outcomes are those changes that are directly linked to some output (*e.g.* a reduction in traffic speeding following a road safety campaign). The intermediate and then final outcomes, say a reduction in accidents and a safer road network, respectively, logically follow (Canadian Institute of Chartered Accountants, 2006).

2.   National "Suites of Indicators" are publications containing key measures of national progress together with some discussion of the links between them, but leaving readers to make their own evaluations of whether the indicators together imply that a country is progressing and, if so, at what rate.

The "suite-of-indicators approach" can be contrasted with the "one-number approach", which combines information about progress across a number of fronts (such as health, wealth and the environment) into a single composite indicator, and the "accounting framework approach", which presents social, economic and environmental data in one unified system of accounts, measured in various units (Trewin and Hall, 2005).

Measuring Australia's Progress sets out the approach clearly: "A reader's assessment of whether Australia is, on balance, progressing will depend on the relative importance he or she places on each dimension. For some readers, an improvement in the health and education of Australians might be more important than a decline in our biodiversity. Others might disagree … The suite of indicators presented in this publication suggests progress in some areas of Australian life and regress in others … Overall progress, as explained above, should not be assessed by simply counting the numbers of areas getting better and subtracting those getting worse. Some aspects of progress (especially aspects such as national income and national wealth) are more easily encapsulated in a small number of indicators, than are some social and environmental aspects. And some readers will give greater importance to some progress indicators than others" (Australian Bureau of Statistics, 2006).

3.   Matthews (2006) points out that higher crime rates, increased pollution, and destruction of natural resources can show up in the GDP as gains. Hurricane Katrina was, therefore, advantageous for the GDP. The Redefining Progress organisation (*www.rprogress.org/*) critiques reliance on GDP as a measure of progress on the basis that, in GDP terms, the hurricane contributed USD$1 billion to the U.S. economy.

The somewhat more refined measures of national income such as GNI (Gross National Income), NNI (Net National Income), or NDP (Net Domestic Product) may be conceptually preferable as measures of well-being, but in practice offer few advantages as they are so closely correlated with GDP that that they lead to a very similar ranking of countries and developments over time.

4.   See: *www.tbs-sct.gc.ca/rma/krc/so-rs_e.asp*.

5.   There is a small body of literature on this term. See Goetz (2001).

6.   See:
www.oecdobserver.org/news/categoryfront.php/id/1269/Spotlight:_Trust_in_go vernment.html

7.   Although Christensen and Lægreid (2003) finds that attitudes formed by political cynicism have the strongest overall effect on variation in people's trust in government.

8.   "Macrobudgetary guidelines set at the beginning of the budgetary process constrain micro-decisions during the remainder of the process. Governments employ hard targets, ceilings, and caps to limit spending; calculate long-term inflationary and program costs through baseline budgeting; enhance program evaluation and financial management systems; create new legislative committees with budgetary oversight responsibilities; establish support agencies to impose greater oversight on the budgetary process; enact budget resolutions and reconciliation devices to control entitlements; and strengthen the powers of finance ministers in constraining spending demands" (Savage, 2005).

9.   Campos and Pradhan (1996) was one of earliest studies on this issue. More recently there has been an extensive array of empirical work. See particularly de Hann *et al.* (1999); Hallerberg *et al.* (2001a); Hallerberg *et al.* (2001b); Poterba and Hagen (1999); von Hagen (1992); von Hagen and Harden (1995); Wanna *et al.* (2003), particularly in relation to EU countries.

Chapter 5. Improving the Measurement of Government Activities

There is a fundamental choice of strategy in building a set of public management indicators. The principal choice is between:

- Starting with a broad-brush approach, gathering aggregate statistics for the key stages in the public sector production process, and working towards some specific analyses.

- Starting with specific, in-depth studies – such as developing unit costs for various public services outputs.

The most frequent request in an international context is for basic benchmarking data, with senior officials seeking insights into how the structures and processes in their country compare to those in other countries. Starting from specific, in-depth studies does not allow benchmarking in the short term. Thus the initial approach to building a public management dataset should most likely entail the collection of a wide array of data, building up to more specific studies – rather than the reverse. In addition, in order to add value and facilitate robust benchmarking, a public management dataset should include information on goods and services produced by the private sector on behalf of the government and should be policy-neutral. It should pursue innovative ways of classifying government inputs, processes and outputs that will ultimately enable policy makers to link public management practices to performance outcomes.

5.1. The scope of data collection

5.1.1. Defining "government"

Public management data should comprise measures of both the market and non-market activities of government and government-owned enterprises. This includes what the System of National Accounts recognises as general government and the government-owned part of the (quasi-) corporate sector, and represents what is traditionally thought of as "government"—ministries, departments, agencies and public corporations at the central and sub-central level. However, data need to also provide insights into other activities which are undertaken outside of core governmental structures and that are completely or partly funded through taxation or other public sector revenues (comprising a new classification of "private sector in the public domain"[1]). This includes private sector organizations that deliver goods and services on behalf of the government, such as for-profit or non-profit hospitals that are accessible to publicly-insured clients.[2] The importance of this domain is its size and the potentially significant contingent fiscal liability that it represents to government.[3]

Table 5.1 sets out the major sites of public sector activity ("institutional domains") that collectively constitute this "public domain". The set of public sector activities summarised in Table 5.1 could be at the core of a future public management data classification system.[4]

5.1.2. Focus on public management rather than policies

The basis for development of public management data is to provide an empirical foundation for understanding the significance and impact of institutional and managerial reforms within the public sector. Such data take government sector policies as a given, and provide information that may assist in illuminating whether these could be implemented more efficiently and how the arrangements for implementation differ between similar arrangements in other countries or over time. It remains important to keep this activity distinct from questions concerning the value of the sector objectives (outcomes) that governments are seeking to achieve.

Table 5.1 Key sites of public management activity[1]

Institutional domain				How transactions are recorded in the National Accounts	Examples
The "public domain"[2]	Public sector	General government[3]	Central government[3]	Administrative units in central government	Ministries and departments in central government
				All non-market non profit-institutions that are controlled and financed by central government units	Schools, hospitals, etc. that are largely funded and controlled by central government but not owned by government
			State governments[3]	Administrative units in state government	Departments in states, provinces
				All non-market non profit-institutions that are controlled and financed by state government units	Schools, hospitals, etc. that are largely funded and controlled by state or provincial government but not owned by government
			Local governments[3]	Administrative units in local government	Departments in counties, municipalities
				All non-market non profit-institutions that are controlled and financed by local government units	Schools, hospitals, etc. that are largely funded and controlled by local government but not owned by government
			Social security funds	All social security funds at each level of government	Health fund, unemployment fund, pension fund
		Public corporations		Market producers, controlled by government, selling goods or services at an economically significant price ("public enterprises"): • Public financial (quasi-) corporations • Public non-financial (quasi-) corporations As defined by S.11 and S.12 in the SNA.	Publicly owned banks Publicly owned harbours, airports, and transportation companies
	Private sector in the public domain[3]			Market producers: • Non-profit institutions • Profit institutions As defined by S.11, S.12 in the SNA	Profit or non-profit private hospitals accessible to publicly insured clients
				Non-profit institutions serving households, financed by government, but not controlled by government: • Non-profit institutions serving households As defined by S.15 in the SNA	Schools, hospitals, etc. that are largely funded by government but not owned nor controlled by government
				Private enterprises with a distinctive and statutorily privileged market position: • Private sector utilities contracted to operate in very limited markets (water, energy, sewage, waste disposal, post, but not telecommunication) • Private sector legal monopolies As defined by S.11 in the SNA	Energy companies and local public transport companies contracted to provide services by public authorities National train company

Notes:

1. This characterisation builds on a framework that has been developed by Dirk-Jan Kraan, Elsa Pilichowski and Edouard Turkisch within the context of OECD work on the questionnaire for the Comparison of Employment in the Public Domain. See OECD (2008).

2. This description has been devised by OECD and is not a recognised SNA term. See OECD (2008).

3. As defined by section S.13 in the System of National Accounts (SNA).

5.2. Establishing a coherent data classification framework

To facilitate benchmarking and the ability to link public management practices to outcomes, data on public management can be classified according to the public sector production process. At a sufficiently high level of generality, there is little disagreement on the four logical steps involved[5] in the public sector production process (see Figure 5.1).

Figure 5.1 The basic public sector production process

Source: Based on Hatry (1999), Pollitt and Bouckaert (2004), and Logic Model Development Guide (2004).

In addition to inputs, activities, outputs and outcomes, there are two other key variables in the process not shown in Figure 5.1: revenues, which contextualize the incentives and constraints governments face in deciding how to produce goods and services, and antecedents or constraints, which contextualise government efficiency and effectiveness.[6] The classification of the public sector production process into these six variables provides a coherent framework and similar units for analysis. When the attributions are clear and, for example, measurable outputs within a given country/sector can be reasonably linked to specific inputs and measurable processes, then the production process is a reasonable way of viewing the data. However, there are many situations where the attribution problems between the stages in Figure 5.1 are so significant that no simple relationship can be identified.[7] When this is the case, these variables are simply measurement categories which can be compared across countries and over time.

The six key variables of the production process comprise numerous data points. Ways in which the data can be disaggregated or broken down to enhance analysis are discussed below.

5.2.1. Inputs[8]

Input measures are important for two reasons: they are a necessity for ratio indicators such as efficiency and cost effectiveness and they may be used as a proxy for output. Inputs in the public sector production process are public expenditures (including tax expenditures) that materialise in different types of physical contributions (labour, goods and services, and capital investment). As such, input data should comprise both financial data (public expenditures including tax expenditures) and non-financial data (such as staff numbers and workforce composition).

Most importantly, input data should be classified in the same way as output data in order to facilitate attribution, distinguishing between the sites of public management activity (Table 5.1). In addition, financial input data could be disaggregated by "mode of production," allowing some analysis of the mix of inputs that were used. One way to accomplish this is to use six categories used in the System of National Accounts: compensation of employees (*i.e.* labour), intermediate consumption (*i.e.* procurement of goods and services), gross capital formation (*i.e.* consumption of fixed capital), social benefits in kind, current transfers and subsidies. Whereas the first three inputs apply to government production, the latter three refer to privatised production wholly or partly funded by government.

For example, in education, the labour (compensation of employees) input consists of the wages and salaries paid to teachers, school secretaries, caretakers and other employees, together with the costs of employing them, such as employer taxes and pension contributions. Intermediate consumption would include expenditures on exercise books, pens, lighting, heating, supply teachers, transport services and items such as data processing services. Gross capital formation includes government expenditures to build schools. Social benefits in kind would include government reimbursements to households who pay for children to attend charter schools or private institutions. Current transfers include monies given to non-profit organizations that provide after-school tutoring services for students. Subsidies are the public contributions to, for instance, private catering companies that provide school meals and to various types of support institutes, such as educational consultancy firms.

This mode of production analysis provides a benchmarking opportunity as it further reveals the preferences of governments concerning the way in which expenditures are utilised to deliver in kind goods and services. In Chapter 2 we made the distinction between easy and hard to measure. Based on the mode of production analysis, we can debate the assumption that complex and hard to measure outputs are more reliably delivered directly by the public sector, while easy to measure, routine based outputs can be more efficiently delivered through outsourcing and contracting with private and not-for-profit providers. Benchmarking these distinctions between countries can lead to a productive debate.

5.2.2. Processes

Public sector processes encompass activities and the overarching structures and institutional arrangements within which these activities occur.

Activities are a key component in converting resources into public value (Moore, 1995), and are constrained or enabled by institutional arrangements (such as the type of public service or the nature of the budgeting and accounting arrangements) and/or the mode of production (such as whether they are produced by government actors or contracted out to the private sector).

Process variables capture key aspects of public management practices and can again be classified by the site of public management activity, or the mode of production (as defined in Table 5.1). Within that classification, the preference is for variables that highlight the existence and application of cross-cutting rules and institutional arrangements, which are easier to identify for "General Government" than for public corporations and private sector entities operating in the public domain. Examples of potential cross-cutting process indicators at the "General Government" level include human resource management arrangements (such as systems determining the degree to which staff move readily in and out of central government employment, arrangements for pay determination and the way in which the very senior staff are managed, including their obligations to avoid conflicts of interest) and rules concerning budget preparation, execution and audit.

On the other hand, arrangements that impact on entities in the "Public Corporations" and "Private Sector in the Public Domain" are more diverse. The key will be to identify the significance of the arrangement, with a preference for data that illuminate processes with the widest possible application.

To the extent feasible, variables that describe significant activities that are likely associated with the quality of hard to measure outputs should be identified separately.

5.2.3. Outputs

Complete data on the production of public goods and services (outputs) encompasses financial data for their value and prices and non-financial data on volume. The methodology used by governments to measure and aggregate public sector outputs is still evolving. Until recently, most countries have estimated output volumes by input volumes due to a lack of data on prices in the National Accounts. The European Commission Decision of 17 December 2002 (2002/990) clarified the principles for the measurement of prices and volumes of government services, and outlawed the use of output indicators based primarily on measuring inputs from 2006.[9] While most European countries have begun measuring the volume of government outputs for health, education and other individual services, only a few countries have begun measuring the volume of government outputs for collective services (such as legislative services and justice) and this is done mainly outside of the National Account statistics.

In order to connect public management inputs, activities and processes to specific outputs, data on all these variables must use the same classification system. For example, if data on inputs and processes are classified according to the sites of public management activity (Table 5.1), then data on outputs should also be collected based on whether the good or service was provided by government entities or the private sector.

Outputs could also be classified according to the basis of measurement (transaction/consumption *vs.* provision), by their use (planning *vs.* accountability and control) and, where appropriate, by the way in which they are used (tight *vs.* loose connection to decision-making). The discussion on the mitigation of gaming problems in Chapter 3 suggests that attention must be paid to the development of independent measures of output quality – through either qualitative interpretation or quantitative measurement of the quality dimensions. In some cases, the quality characteristic of the output can best be measured by examining the degree to which the outputs have contributed to outcomes. Over time, variables capturing outputs could be associated with data concerning the degree to which they are accompanied by independent measures of output quality, of quality management and assurance arrangements, and of the frequency with which the measures are changed.

As noted earlier, government also provides regulatory services. Regulatory output is intangible and unmeasurable other than via very crude proxies (number of new regulations, number of pages of regulatory materials, etc.). Thus regulatory activity can best be measured by examining, on the one hand, the processes for generating and managing the regulations and, on the other, the outcomes (the effect of regulations on the key economic and social sectors).

5.2.4. Outcomes

Outcome indicators should focus on public management outcomes rather than policy sector outcomes such as educational attainment, life expectancy and air quality. Chapter 4 suggested that consideration be given to identifying a set of "executive governance outcomes" which are primarily related to the activities of the executive branch of government.

"Executive governance outcomes" might be broadly of three types: public confidence, equity and fiscal/economic stability. Public confidence might encompass issues around trust in government, and associated concerns relating to the predictability and acceptability of government policy. Equity might encompass the measured distribution of services and benefits across diverse populations. Fiscal and economic stability might relate to the track record of government in these spheres.

In relation to trust, the survey data currently available offering limited international comparability due in part to conceptual uncertainties in relation to the question that they are addressing. A consistent data set would allow some movement towards assessing institutional effectiveness – addressing the question of which reforms of structures and processes really are associated with concrete changes in particular aspects of trust.

There is little direct connection between public management outcomes and the sites of public management activity (Table 5.1) as outcomes generally depend on a multiplicity of actors.

5.2.5. Antecedents or constraints

Relatively little research has been conducted on understanding direct linkages between a country's political context and the inputs, processes, outputs and outcomes of public administration. Public administration research concentrates on the machinery of government, often taking the political context as given. However, by determining what views are represented in government, how policy decisions are made and by whom and who administers programs and reforms, a country's political context can clearly affect laws and institutional arrangements and ultimately public sector efficiency and effectiveness. Important contextual factors include core public sector values, electoral systems and coalition governments, executive and legislative power and administrative structures—including the division of responsibilities horizontally (between departments and ministries) and vertically (across levels of governments). Situating policies and indicators within this contextual background can help us better understand differences between countries.

5.2.6. Revenues[10]

In considering the public sector, it is also important to look at the revenue arrangements. Examining how government raises its revenues (taxation, fees, property income, transfers, and the incurrence of public debt) will provide insights into the incentives and constraints that governments face in determining how to provide goods and services. Public revenues are commonly distinguished as tax and non-tax revenues. Non-tax revenues can further be distinguished in fees (charges for the use of public services), property income (proceeds from the sale or rent of property), concessions (payment for the right to exploit a natural resource or public monopoly), and transfers. The revenue data could also include the incurrence of public debt and the stock of public debt, the latter being a measure of future taxation required for debt redemption.

5.3. OECD's role

5.3.1. Data collection

Data collection and indicator development should build on the areas in which the OECD's Public Governance Committee has some recognised competence, which would imply that the OECD should continue to focus on the machinery of government as opposed to sector outputs and outcomes. The public management data collected by the OECD has focused historically on data concerning public sector processes, as these are institutional and managerial concerns. Core OECD data includes indicators on government revenue and expenditure structures; employment and compensation in the public domain; and institutional arrangements such as budget procedures, HRM practices, performance management and e-government. The available data can be roughly classified as shown in Table 5.2.

Table 5.2 Currently available data

REVENUES	
Sub-central government	Revenue structure
	Tax autonomy (for selected countries; no time series available)
	Grants (for selected countries; no time series available)
	Fiscal rules (for selected countries; no time series available)
INPUTS	
Overall input mix	
Labour	Workforce size
	Workforce composition
	Compensation
PROCESSES	
Budget practices and procedures	System overview
	Budget formulation
	Budget execution
	Reporting, review and audit
HRM arrangements	System overview
	Pay policy
	Ethical infrastructure and oversight
Internal and external reporting	Open government
	Performance measurement arrangements
E-government readiness	
Centre of government	Government offices
Management of regulatory quality	

Source: OECD (2007).

Continued collection of this core dataset will provide time-series data that enables a broader analysis of the effects of public sector reforms and trends in management processes. In addition, the OECD should gradually expand its datasets to include indicators on the quality of public sector processes.

In considering outputs, there are potentially three types of indicators of service quality that OECD can explore: equity in access to services; user-friendliness of services; and citizen satisfaction with their treatment and the services provided. Initial efforts may focus on whether countries have systems for assessing service quality, with OECD eventually collecting data in a comparative framework.

Internationally comparable output and outcome data are scarce and, as noted in Table 5.2, the OECD does not currently collect data on outputs and outcomes. However, given the OECD's unique role as a forum of public sector administrators from over 30 countries, it can work to build consensus amongst its member nations over appropriate measures of public administration outputs and outcomes of public and, over time, can begin to collect data.

5.3.2. Emphasis on data quality and transparency

The network of OECD countries drives an institutional focus on data quality and transparency. While there are other bodies and institutions that develop useful public management datasets, the OECD could differentiate itself by establishing a reputation for quality such that inclusion of a dataset is a badge of honour. This requires establishing a clear data quality threshold for inclusion, ensuring consistency in the units of analysis, maximising opportunities for others to propose data and encouraging particular collection efforts to cover key data gaps. As shown in Box 5.1, the OECD already has a framework for data quality in place that can be applied to the public management dataset. In addition, the OECD could set an international standard for transparency by providing open access to raw data, encouraging a meaningful dialogue within and among countries and in academic and policy spheres.

Box 5.1 Compliance with the OECD Quality Framework for Statistical Activities

OECD defines data quality as "fitness for use" in terms of user needs. This definition is broader than has been customarily used in the past when quality was equated with accuracy. It is now generally recognised that there are other important dimensions and quality is recognised as a multi-faceted concept. The OECD Quality Framework for Statistical activities (OECD, 2003b) comprises seven dimensions, which can be summarised as follows:

- *Relevance* of data products is a qualitative assessment of the degree to which they serve the purposes for which they are sought by users. Data can be well-recognised in the field and cited in government reports (high policy relevance) or little used beyond academic papers (lower policy relevance).

- *Accuracy* is the degree to which the data correctly estimate or describe the quantities or characteristics they are designed to measure. Data can derive from well-accepted classifications and procedures, validated by reference to independent data sources (high quality) or from *ad hoc* classifications and procedures with no cross-checking against other data (lower quality).

- *Credibility* refers to the confidence that users place in the data. It is determined in part by the integrity of the process through which the data is generated. Data can be based on standard, replicable procedures capturing unambiguous data (highly objective), or include survey-based data (less objective) or expert assessments (least objective).

- *Timeliness* reflects the length of time between data availability and the event or phenomenon they describe. Key questions include: are time series available, how frequently is the data produced, and what is the planned future availability of the data?

- *Interpretability* concerns the ease with which the user may understand and properly use and analyse the data. It is determined in part by the adequacy of the definitions of concepts, variables and terminology, information describing the limitations of the data. Key questions include: do the questions have the same meaning for all countries, and is the underlying data clearly defined?

- *Coherence* is the degree to which data are logically connected and mutually consistent – within a dataset, across datasets, over time and across countries.

- *Accessibility* reflects how readily the data can be located and accessed. Key considerations include the source of information and the ease with which the user can gain access to the data.

5.3.3. Co-ordinate efforts

As governments and the international community devote more resources to measuring government activity, the OECD can play a unique role in co-ordinating these efforts. While the OECD will continue to undertake some data collection in core areas – as it has a distinct comparative advantage in its access to governments – it will be necessary to combine this data collection role with an increased emphasis on networking with other bodies and institutions that develop public management datasets. Combining the OECD's unique convening power with a clearer specification of technical standards and identification of data gaps will encourage other data suppliers to work on priority areas and conform to OECD standards. This may have the additional advantage of minimising overlapping survey demands on OECD member countries' government time.

Notes

1. This description has been devised specifically for this purpose and is not a recognised SNA term.

2. The SNA contains financial data describing transfers from the general government to other units. However, the data are reported for all units—not necessarily for those that receive more than 50% of their financing from the government.

3. The term "significant" is important here. There is no assumption that government will automatically assume all financial responsibilities for all activities encompassed by Table 10 in the event of some service failure. The key public management data are those which relate to those activities which are politically important and therefore are most likely to represent such a liability, but there is no certainty.

4. This is consistent with the approach proposed in Gallais (2006).

5.   Noting that there is far less consensus on the socio-economic objectives that lead to the selection of desired outcomes, as this is a matter of normative economics and political preferences.

6.   There is a rather daunting literature on the finer points of classification. Schick highlights this somewhat obsessive concern with arcane questions: "(o)ne of the curious features of this (performance) literature is the endless arguing over what is an output and an outcome; whether a particular measure is an end outcome or an intermediate outcome; whether goals, objectives and targets mean the same things or are different" (Schick, 2005). The issue is clearly not resolvable in any absolute sense – and it is not evident that there is much return on a major discussion of these fine points. Boyle (2005) provides one of the more succinct and pragmatic approaches to these questions.

7.   See Gregory (1995) for one of the more passionate arguments about the risks of forcing all government activities into a production mode, arguing that it denies the reality that many public sector activities are, in the terms of Wilson (1989), either "craft" (in which outcomes can be observed but not outputs such as many police or social work tasks) or "coping" (in which neither outcomes or outputs can be observed, such as the diplomatic service).

8.   This section draws significantly on Atkinson *et al.* (2005).

9.   This change in the basis for measuring outputs is particularly well-explained in Lequiller (2005).

10.   This section draws significantly on Atkinson *et al.* (2005).

Annex A. Co-ordinating with Data Collection Developments in Non-OECD Countries

Non-OECD middle and high income countries[1]

The collection and publication of public management data in the OECD could usefully be replicated in non-OECD middle and high income countries for two main reasons. First, there is a potential direct benefit. The public sector reform efforts of these countries can be intrinsically similar to those of the OECD, focusing on second order challenges which build on an entrenched discipline in the behaviour of civil servants and an organisational culture of following the rules.[2] The possibility of benchmarking themselves against key developments in OECD member countries is likely to be attractive, providing a spur to country efforts on public sector improvement. Although middle income countries, by definition, have higher per capita incomes, a third of the world's poor (people living on less than USD$1 a day) live in middle income countries.[3] Improving the efficiency and effectiveness of the public sector in these settings is an essential component of poverty reduction.

There is also an indirect benefit. The point is often made, with justification, that public management concerns are downstream from the over-arching governance problems that limit development. Issues such as weak parliamentary oversight, opaque arrangements for political party financing, media with low capacity or facing government restrictions and providing the public with limited access to information concerning the performance of government, are identified as the primary obstacles to development – with public management in effect a dependent rather than independent variable. The difficulty with this analysis is that it does not suggest where or how traction might be gained. The advantage of a structured exchange between senior practitioners on public management issues is that it provides an entry point to a dialogue with the most senior officials, opening up opportunities for broader governance and policy discussions. Also indirectly, as many of the non-OECD middle income countries are the beneficiaries of various forms of technical assistance and partnership arrangements with OECD member countries, comparable public management indicators would assist in providing a common basis for dialogue concerning the focus of this assistance.

Special attention will be paid to countries that are currently under review for accession to the OECD, namely Chile, Estonia, Israel, Russia and Slovenia and countries that the OECD have enhanced engagement activities: Brazil, China, India and Indonesia

---

Box 1A.1 OECD collaboration on public sector reform with middle and high income (non-OECD) countries

China (Lower middle-income economy)

Collaboration between China and the OECD on public governance issues was initiated 10 years ago. In 2003-2005, the OECD conducted policy dialogue with China on the impact of governance on the efficiency and effectiveness of public action in 10 policy areas: labour policies, the banking sector, competition, intellectual property rights, foreign investment, statistics, corporate governance and the management of state assets, agriculture, environmental protection and higher education. Collaboration is continuing in relation to public administration, regulatory reform, and regional development and multi-level governance.

Brazil (Lower middle-income economy)

The OECD has undertaken extensive outreach work in the region in general, including on integrity and budget reforms. Brazil is now requesting more focused assistance on public sector efficiency and the OECD is responding.

Russian Federation (Upper middle-income economy)

OECD collaboration with the Russian Federation includes key issues in modernisation of government, particularly regulatory reform, budget reform and management of the senior civil service.

Governance for Development Initiative in the Middle East and North Africa (including lower middle-income economies: Algeria, Egypt (Arab Republic), Iran (Islamic Republic), Iraq, Jordan, Morocco, Syrian Arab Republic, Tunisia, West Bank & Gaza; Upper middle-income (non-OECD) economies: Lebanon; High-income (non-OECD) economies: Bahrain, Qatar, Saudi Arabia and the United Arab Emirates)

OECD outreach work is resulting in a series of practitioner networks on specific institutional areas (public expenditure, civil service and integrity, regulatory reform, e-government). A recent ministerial level meeting in Sharm El Sheikh has provided strong political support for the activity which is now developing, with the World Bank and other donors, some regional capacity building seminars and selected country pilot projects.

Regional Network of Senior Budget Officials (SBO)

Regional SBO networks have been established in Asia, Latin America and Eastern Europe that bring together the budget directors from the respective regions. These practitioner networks replicate the *modus operandi* of the core SBO for member countries. As part of the regional networks, peer reviews of the budgeting systems of countries in the respective region are undertaken in a similar manner to that done for member countries.

As data collection efforts grow in profile and coverage within the OECD, it is probable that interest from non-OECD member countries in contributing will grow in step. Interest could be spurred by the establishment of a challenge fund, or similar arrangement, which could co-finance the start-up costs of collecting and contributing data for countries which demonstrate a clear business plan for developing and using public sector data.[4]

In parallel, attempts will be made to include data coverage for middle income countries. Initially focusing on Brazil, the Russian Federation, India and China – but subsequently broadening to other middle income countries. Initial focus of the data for these countries is likely to be core public sector processes (fiscal and budgetary management, ethical infrastructure and oversight, centre of government structures and modes of production).

Low income countries

For low income countries, various public management indicators are under development by the World Bank and partners. As examples:

- The Public Expenditure and Financial Accountability (PEFA) programme uses 28 indicators to track public financial management (2006). These indicators track a combination of processes (comprehensiveness and transparency, quality of the budget cycle), intermediate outcomes (variance between actual expenditures and revenues and original approved budget, level of and changes in expenditure arrears), and antecedents or constraints (elements of donor practices which impact the performance of country public financial management systems).

- The Doing Business Surveys track various processes and intermediate outcomes, including the regulatory procedures for starting a business and obtaining licenses, registering property, paying taxes and cross-border trading (World Bank and International Finance Corporation, 2006).

- The Investment Climate Surveys (*http://rru.worldbank.org/EnterpriseSurveys/*) also provide data on processes and intermediate outcomes including senior management time spent dealing with requirements of regulations, consistency in interpretations of regulations, reported corruption, time spent in meetings with tax officials, time to clear direct exports through customs.

- There is growing interest within the World Bank and other donor agencies in the development of a newer range of "actionable" public management and other governance indicators.[5] The World Bank has obtained funding for development work and data collection in a particular range of low income countries (essentially those with a per capita income in 2004 of less than USD$965). There is some emphasis on human resource management indicators.

The focus of the public sector processes and outcomes under study in low income countries, and the purpose of the resulting indicators, is very different from the situation in the OECD. In low income countries, donors are looking for evidence of improvements in first order concerns such as reductions in large-scale corruption and in the institutionalisation of basic budgetary and HRM systems.

The opportunity for collaboration with these World Bank and other initiatives for low income countries is primarily at the level of the data collection framework. To the extent that some low income countries will graduate from that category, as the combined result of higher per capita incomes and more robust public sectors, then consistency in the broad categories of data tracked would allow some continuity in monitoring.

Notes

1. The World Bank classifies countries by income group: Economies are divided according to 2004 GNI per capita, calculated using the World Bank Atlas method. The groups are: low income, USD$935 or less; lower middle income, USD$936 - 3 705; upper middle income, USD$3 706 - 11 455; and high income, USD$11 456 or more.

   Annex 2 provides a more complete list. See *http://siteresources.worldbank.org/DATASTATISTICS/Resources/CLASS.X LS* for the full classification as at 1 July 2005.

Classification by income does not necessarily reflect development status and the OECD DAC classifications identify Least Developed Countries separately, based on UN definitions.

2. This is in distinction to first order reforms, typically faced by low income countries, which are intended to achieve or strengthen public sector discipline. Manning and Parison (2003) explores this distinction in more detail.

3. See World Bank (2006)

4. As an example, in the UK Department for International Development Challenge Funds, bids (essentially comprising costed proposals for assistance showing how additional funds would complement government efforts) are invited for a centrally managed fixed sum. The bids received by a widely advertised closing date are evaluated on their technical merits and on the basis of the sustainability of the effort after the grant has been utilised. The evaluation is undertaken by an independent panel and is undertaken in two stages. Stage 1 confirms that the criteria are met, more detailed proposals submitted in stage 2 are then evaluated and winning proposals selected by the panel. Bidding is competitive and grants are allocated according to the degree to which bids met the scheme criteria and objectives. See *www.challengefunds.org/index.htm*.

5. "Governance should be monitored regularly. To complement existing aggregate indicators, additional effort is needed to monitor specific, actionable indicators, such as quality of public financial management, procurement practices, and checks and balances. This monitoring can help to track progress, generate greater accountability, and build demand for good governance. It can also help underpin long-term dialog between countries and development partners, to develop realistic goals and sequencing of governance reforms" (International Monetary Fund and World Bank, 2006). The discussion of aggregate governance indicators above provides some assessment of the existing range of broad governance indicators.

Annex B. Outcome Measures of Well-being Included in at Least Two National Publications Tracking Government Performance[1]

INDICATORS	Australia	Canada	Finland	New Zealand	Switzerland	United kingdom	EUROSTAT
1.Health	✓	✓	✓	✓	✓	✓	✓
1.1.Life expectancy at birth/healthy life expectancy	✓	✓	·	✓	✓	✓	✓
1.1.1.Incidence of all cancer/skin cancer	✓	·	✓		·	·	✓
1.1.2.Infant mortality rate	✓	✓	·		·	·	·
1.2.Obesity	·	·	✓	✓	·	✓	✓
1.3.Expenditure on prevention and health promotion	·	·	·	·	✓	·	✓
2. Education & training	✓	✓	✓	✓	✓	✓	✓
2.1. Public expenditure on education as a % GDP	·	·	·	·	✓	·	✓
2.2. Education levels	·	✓	✓	·	·	✓	·
2.3. Educational attainment of the adult population	·	✓		✓	·	·	·
2.4. Adult literacy	·	✓	·	✓	·	·	·
3.Work	✓	✓	✓	✓	✓	✓	✓
3.1.Unemployment rate	✓	·	✓	✓	✓	·	·
3.2.Employment rate	·	✓	·	✓	·	✓	✓
4.National income	✓	✓	✓	✓	✓	✓	✓
4.1.Real net national disposable income per capita	✓	·	·	✓	·	·	·
4.1.1.Real GDP per capita	✓	✓	·	·	✓	·	·
4.2.Investment as % of GDP, by institutional sector	·	·	·	·	✓	✓	✓
4.3.Inflation rate	·	·	✓	·	·	·	✓
5.Financial hardship	✓	·	✓	✓	✓	✓	✓
5.1.Inequality of income distribution	·	·	·	·	✓	·	✓
6.Housing	✓	✓	·	✓	✓	✓	✓

INDICATORS	Australia	Canada	Finland	New Zealand	Switzerland	United kingdom	EUROSTAT
7.Productivity	✓	✓	✓	·	✓	✓	✓
7.1.Labour productivity	✓	·	·	·	✓	·	✓
7.2.Expenditure on R&D	✓	·	✓	·	✓	·	✓
8.The natural landscape	✓	·	✓	·	✓	✓	✓
8.1.Threatened species trend	✓	·	·	·	·	·	✓
8.2.Fish stocks	✓	·	✓	·	·	✓	·
8.3.Forest resources	·	·	✓	·	✓	·	·
8.4.Biodiversity	·	·	·	·	✓	✓	·
9.The human environment	✓	✓	✓	✓	✓	✓	✓
9.1.Air quality	·	✓	✓	✓	·	·	·
9.2.Emissions of air pollutants	·	·	·	·	·	✓	✓
10. International environmental concerns	✓	✓	✓	·	✓	✓	✓
10.1.Net greenhouse gas emissions	✓	·	✓	·	✓	✓	·
10.2.Thickness of ozone layer	·	·	✓	·	✓	·	·
10.3.Mean temperatures	·	·	✓	·	✓	·	·
11. Family community and social cohesion	✓	✓	✓	✓	✓	✓	·
11.1.Suicide and drug-induced death rates	✓	·	✓	✓	✓	·	✓
12.Crime	✓	✓	✓	✓	✓	✓	·
12.1.Violent and drug crime	·	·	✓	·	✓	·	·
12.2.Killed and injured persons in road traffic	·	·	·	✓	✓	✓	✓
13.Governance, democracy and citizenship	✓	✓	✓	✓	·	·	✓
13.1.Voter turnout and informal votes cast	✓	·	·	✓	·	·	·
13.2.Women in Federal Parliament	✓	·	·	✓	✓	·	·
14. Cultural identity	·	·	✓	✓	✓	·	·
14.1.Attendance at cultural events	·	·	·	✓	✓	·	·
15.Transport	·	·	✓	·	✓	✓	✓
15.1.Modal split of passenger transport	·	·	·	·	✓	·	✓
15.2.Modal split of freight transport	·	·	·	·	✓	·	✓
15.3.Road length	·	·	✓	·	✓	·	·
16.Global Partnership	·	✓	✓	·	✓	✓	✓
16.1.ODA	·	✓	✓	·	✓	·	·
17. Energy	·	·	✓	·	✓	✓	✓

Sources: *Australia*: Australian Bureau of Statistics (ABS), Measures of Australia's Progress; *Canada*: Treasury Board of Canada Secretariat, Canada's Performance, 2004; *EUROSTAT*: European Commission, Sustainable Development Indicators to monitor the implementation of the EU Sustainable Development Strategy SEC (2005) 161 final; *Finland*: Finnish Sustainable Development Indicators 2003, Finnish National Commission on Sustainable Development, Finnish Ministry of the Environment; *New Zealand*: Statistics New Zealand, The Social Report 2005; *Switzerland*: Monitoring Sustainable Development, MONET, Final Report Methods and Results, Swiss Federal Statistical Office, 2004; *United Kingdom*: The UK Government Sustainable Development Strategy, 2005.

Note

1.   Developed from original work by Ayhan Uysal, OECD, Statistics Directorate.

Glossary

Term	Use in *Measuring Government Activity*	Formal meaning
Aggregate indicator	See composite indicator.	"Aggregation denotes the compounding of primary data into an aggregate, usually for the purpose of expressing them in a summary form" (OECD, 2004).
Composite indicator	An indicator formed by compiling individual indicators into a single index on the basis of an underlying model (Nardo *et al.*, 2005).	Strictly speaking, if the individual indicators are combining different measures of a similar concept within the single measure, the result is an aggregate measure (see *www.undp.org/oslocentre/cross_faq.htm*). However, for simplicity, all such compiled measures are referred to in this note as composite indicators.
Contingent liabilities	"Significant" liabilities which may be explicit (where the government is legally mandated to settle the obligation when it becomes due) or Implicit (the obligation is based on public expectations and political pressures).	"Obligations that have been entered into, but the timing and amount of which are contingent on the occurrence of some uncertain future event. They are therefore not yet liabilities, and may never be if the specific contingency does not materialise" (see *www.imf.org/external/np/fad/trans/manual/glos s.htm*. See also Polackova, 1999).
Dataset	A set of indicators or variables concerning a single topic (*e.g.* regulatory quality).	A permanently stored collection of information relating to a single subject (OECD, 2004).
Derived indicator	An indicator produced on the basis of other indicators by a procedure other than through simple compilation or aggregation.	"A derived statistic is obtained by an arithmetical observation from the primary observations. In this sense, almost every statistic is 'derived'. The term is mainly used to denote descriptive statistical quantities obtained from data which are primary in the sense of being mere summaries of observations, *e.g.* population figures are primary and so are geographical areas, but population-per-square-mile is a derived quantity" (OECD, 2004).

Terms	Use in *Measuring Government Activity*	Formal meaning
Efficiency	Costs per unit of output.	In economics efficiency is used in two ways: operational or technical efficiency and allocative efficiency. Operational efficiency is costs per unit of output, given the existing input combination. Allocative (input) efficiency is costs per unit of output, given the input prices. The efficient input combination may change according to a change in input prices. Cost efficiency comprises both operational and allocative (input) efficiency (Coelli *et al.*, 1999).
Final (end) outcome	The impacts on, or the consequences for, the community of the outputs or activities of government. Outcomes significantly reflect the intended or unintended results of government actions, but other factors are also implicated.	The final result desired from delivering outputs. An output may have more than one end outcome; or several outputs may contribute to a single end outcome. (*http://www.ssc.govt.nz/Glossary/*) See also OECD (2002).
Financial input	Costs of inputs financed by expenditures or tax expenditures.	Costs at current prices of the inputs sacrificed to produce outputs (Atkinson *et al.*, 2005).
Financial proxy output	Value of outputs or groups of outputs, measured by input costs.	The value of non-market output can be estimated directly or indirectly. The conventional method for the government is indirect, namely by the "input method ", which consists of measuring output value by the sum of input costs sacrificed for its production (SNA, 1993).
Gaming	A conscious response to manipulate outputs or data as a reaction to measurement.	"(R)eactive subversion such as 'hitting the target and missing the point' or reducing performance where targets do not apply" (Bevan and Hood, 2005).
Indicator	A variable that contributes to analysis.	"… quantitative or a qualitative measure derived from a series of observed facts that can reveal relative positions (*e.g.* of a country) in a given area. When evaluated at regular intervals, an indicator can point out the direction of change across different units and through time" (Nardo *et al.*, 2005).

Terms	Use in *Measuring Government Activity*	Formal meaning
Input (non-financial)	Units of labour, capital, goods and services sacrificed for the production of services.	"Taking the health service as an example, input is defined as the time of medical and non-medical staff, the drugs, the electricity and other inputs purchased, and the capital services from the equipment and buildings used" (Lequiller, 2005).
Intermediate outcome	A consequence of the outputs or activities of government which contributes towards the final outcome. Can be more directly attributed to public sector activities than final outcomes.	An intermediate outcome is expected to lead to an end outcome, but, in itself, is not the desired result (*http://www.ssc.govt.nz/Glossary/*).
Mode of production classification	The key classifications proposed for future data collection are: intermediate consumption (contracting out and procurement), compensation of employees, gross capital expenditure, social benefits in kind, and subsidies. These are the main inputs in the economic classification.	Disaggregation of expenditures into categories reflecting how the public sector uses these expenditures to produce goods and services.
Non-financial output measures	Output measures derived from the direct measurement of output volume and associated quality characteristics.	Measures which arise from "the calculation of a volume indicator of output using appropriately weighted measures of output of the various categories of non-market goods and services produced" (Lequiller, 2005).
Output (non-financial)	Output derived from the direct measurement of output volume and associated quality characteristics.	Measures which arise from "the calculation of a volume indicator of output using appropriately weighted measures of output of the various categories of non-market goods and services produced" (Lequiller, 2005).
Performance	Used **non-analytically** to convey that achievements matter as well as probity and parsimony in resource use.	The term "performance" is used to indicate that there is a standard to which managers, agencies will be held to account – beyond complying with constraints on the consumption of inputs.[1] The difficulty in the term is that the standard that is to be achieved can refer to anything at all beyond inputs – whether it is in fact classifiable as processes, outputs, or outcomes.

Terms	Use in *Measuring Government Activity*	Formal meaning
Productivity	Output per unit of input or weighted inputs.	Economists distinguish between total productivity, namely total output divided by total (weighted) input(s) and marginal productivity, namely change in output divided by change in (weighted) input(s) (Coelli *et al.*, 1999).
Public sector process	Structures, procedures and management arrangements with a broad application within the public sector.	Cross-cutting managerial and institutional arrangements within the public sector (Andersen, 2004).
Value	The numerical measure or a category assigned to a particular variable (can mean worth but only when this is clear from the context).	A data element value is a value out of a set of permissible values pertaining to a data element. Alternatively, value at the level of a single, homogeneous good or service is equal to the price per unit of quantity multiplied by the number of quantity units of that good or service; in contrast to price, value is independent of the choice of quantity unit (OECD, 2004).
Variable	A characteristic of a unit (often it is equivalent to an answer to a single question in an OECD survey).	A variable is a characteristic of a unit being observed that may assume more than one of a set of values to which a numerical measure or a category from a classification can be assigned (*e.g.* income, age, weight, etc., and "occupation", "industry", "disease", etc.) (OECD, 2004).

1. For example, "Performance-based management is a systematic approach to performance improvement through an ongoing process of establishing strategic performance objectives; measuring performance; collecting, analyzing, reviewing, and reporting performance data; and using that data to drive performance improvement" (Artley *et al.*, 2001).

Bibliography

Afonso, A., L. Schuknecht and V. Tanzi. 2006. *Public Sector Efficiency: Evidence for New EU Member States and Emerging Markets*. Frankfurt: European Central Bank.

Algemene Rekenkamer. 2006. *Performance Audit Manual*. The Hague: European Affairs & Government-wide Performance Audit Division, Netherlands Court of Audit.

Ammons, D.N. 2003. "Performance and Managerial Thinking". *Public Performance and Management Review*. 25 (4). 344-7.

Andersen, K. 2004. *E-Government and Public Sector Process Rebuilding*. New York: Kluwer.

Andrews, R., G. Boyne. and R. Walker. 2006. "Subjective and Objective Measures of Organizational Performance: An Empirical Exploration" in Boyne, G.; Meier, K.; O'Toole Jr., L. and Walker, R. (eds.) *Public Service Performance: Perspectives on Measurement and Management*, Cambridge, United Kingdom: Cambridge University Press. 14-34.

Arndt, C. and C. Oman. 2006. *Uses and Abuses of Governance Indicators*. Paris: OECD Development Centre.

Anielski, M. 2002. *A Sustainability Accounting System for Canada*. Research paper prepared for the National Round Table on the Environment and the Economy, June 15, 2002.

Artley, W., D.J. Ellison and B. Kennedy. 2001. *The Performance-Based Management Handbook – Volume 1: Establishing and Maintaining a Performance-Based Management Program*. Washington, D.C.: Training Resources and Data Exchange (Performance-Based Management Special Interest Group).

Atkinson, T., J. Grice, A. Simkins, L. de Freitas, J. Hemingway, B. King, P. Lee, M. Lyon, N. Mai, S. Mehmi, A. Pritchard, J. Snelling, A. Tuke, L. Watson and G. Fletcher-Cooke. 2005. *Measurement of Government Output and Productivity for the National Accounts*. Basingstoke: Palgrave.

Auluck, R. 2002. "Benchmarking: A Tool for Facilitating Organizational Learning". *Public Administration and Development*. 2002 (22). 109-22.

Australian Bureau of Statistics. 2006. *Measuring Australia's Progress*. Canberra: Australian Bureau of Statistics.

Australian National Audit Office. 2001. *Performance Information in Portfolio Budget Statements*. Canberra: ANAO.

Babb, P. 2005. "Measurement of Social Capital in the UK". In *Statistics, Knowledge and Policy: Key Indicators to Inform Decision Making*. Paris: OECD. 532-535.

Barclay, G. and C. Tavares. 2003. *International Comparisons of Criminal Justice Statistics 2001 - Home Office Statistical Bulletin*, Issue 12/03. London: Home Office.

Barnes, C. and D. Gill. 2000. *Declining Government Performance? Why Citizens Don't Trust Government*. Wellington: State Services Commission.

Behn, R. and P. Kant. 1999. "Strategies for Avoiding the Pitfalls of Performance Contracting". *Public Productivity and Management Review*. 22 (4). 470–89.

Bellefeuille-Prégent, L. and T. Wilson. 2005. "Societal Indicators and Government-Wide Reporting in the Government of Canada". *Statistics, Knowledge and Policy: Key Indicators to Inform Decision Making*. Paris: OECD. 306-318.

Berliner, J. S. 1956. "A Problem in Soviet Business Administration". *Administrative Science Quarterly*. 1 (1). 86-102.

Besançon, M.. 2003. "Good Governance Rankings: The Art of Measurement". *World Peace Foundation*. Cambridge, Massachusetts: John F. Kennedy School of Government, Harvard University

Bevan, G. and C. Hood. 2006. "What's Measured Is What Matters: Targets and Gaming in the English Public Health Care System". *Public Administration*. 84:3. 517-538.

Biase, L de. 2005. "Agree on Numbers While Discussing Words. Or Is It Just the Opposite?" in *Statistics, Knowledge and Policy: Key Indicators to Inform Decision Making*. Paris: OECD. 494-500.

Bird, R. 2004. "Administrative Dimensions of Tax Reform." *Asia-Pacific Tax Bulletin* (March 2004). 134-50.

Bird, S., D. Cox, V. Farewell, H. Goldstein, T. Holt and P. Smith. 2005. "Performance Indicators: Good, Bad, and Ugly". *Journal of the Royal Statistical Society: Series A (Statistics in Society)*. 168 (1). 1-27.

Blankart, C. 1987. "Limits to Privatization". *European Economic Review (Netherlands)*. 31 (February/March). 346-51.

Boarini, R., A. Johansson and M. Mira d'Ercole. 2006. "Alternative Measures of Well-Being". *OECD Social, Employment and Migration Working Paper No. 33*. Paris: OECD.

Bok, D. 1997. "Measuring the Performance of Government" in S. Nye, P. D. Zelikow and D. C. King (eds.) *Why People Don't Trust Government*. Cambridge, Massachusetts: Harvard University Press. 55-76.

Bos, F. 2003. "The National Accounts as a Tool for Analysis and Policy: Past, Present and Future". PhD Thesis. Enschede: Twente University.

Boston, J. 2000. "The Challenge of Evaluating Systemic Change: The Case of Public Management Reform". *International Public Management Journal*. 3 (1). 23-46.

Bouckaert, G. 1995. "Measuring Quality" in C. Pollitt and G. Bouckaert (eds.) *Quality Improvement in European Public Services. Concepts, Cases and Commentary*. London: Sage Publications. 22-32.

Bouckaert, G. and W. Balk. 1991. "Public Productivity Measurement: Diseases and Cures". *Public Productivity and Management Review*. 15 (2). 229-35.

Bouckaert, G. and A. Halachmi. 1995. "The Range of Performance Indicators in the Public Sector: Theory Versus Practice" in Halachmi, A. and D. Grant. *Reengineering and Performance Measurement in Criminal Justice Social Programmes*. Perth: IIAS. 91-106.

Bouckaert, G., P. Lægreid and S. Van de Walle. 2005. "Trust, Quality Measurement Models, and Value Chain Monitoring: Symposium Introduction". *Public Performance and Management Review*. 28 (4). 460-4.

Bouckaert, G. and S. Van de Walle. 2003. "Quality of Public Service Delivery and Trust in Government" in A. Salminen (ed.) *Governing Networks: AGPE Yearbook*. Amsterdam, Netherlands: IOS Press.

Boyle, R. 2005. *Civil Service Performance Indicators*. Dublin: Institute of Public Administration.

Boyne, G., C. Farrell, J. Law, M. Powell and R. Walker. 2003. *Evaluating Public Management Reforms*. Buckingham: Open University Press.

Boyne, G. and J. Law. 2004. "Designing Performance Measurements to Be Drawn on in the Second Generation of Local Public Service Agreements (Local PSAs)". Unpublished draft. London: Office of the Deputy Prime Minister.

Boyne, G., K. Meier, L. O'Toole Jr. and R. Walker (eds.) *Public Service Performance: Perspectives on Measurement and Management*, Cambridge, United Kingdom: Cambridge University Press.

Breeman, G. 2003. "Explaining Failures of Regaining Public Trust: The Case of Agricultural Policy-Formation in the Netherlands". Paper presented on the EGPA Annual Conference, Oeiras 3-6 September 2003. Oeiras, Portugal: EGPA.

Burgess, S., C. Propper and D. Wilson. 2002. *Does Performance Monitoring Work? A Review of the Evidence from the UK Public Sector, Excluding Health Care (CMPO Working Paper Series No. 02/49)*. Bristol, United Kingdom: The Centre for Market and Public Organisation.

Campos, E. and S. Pradhan. 1996. *Budgetary Institutions and Expenditure Outcomes (Policy Research Working Paper No. 1646)*. Washington, D.C.: World Bank.

Carter, N., R. Klein and P. Day. 1992. *How Organizations Measure Success: The Use of Performance Indicators in Government*. London, Routledge.

Chan, M., M. Nizette, L. La Rance, C. Broughton and D. Russell. 2002. "Australia". *OECD Journal on Budgeting*. 1 (4). 35-69.

Chanley, V.A., T.J. Rudolph and W.M. Rahn. 2000. "The Origins and Consequences of Public Trust in Government: A Time Series Analysis". *Public Opinion Quarterly*. 64 (3).

Cheung, P. 2005. "Millennium Development Goals: Measuring and Monitoring Global Progress", in *Statistics, Knowledge and Policy: Key Indicators to Inform Decision Making*. Paris: OECD. 374-84.

Christensen, T. and P. Lægreid. 2003. "Trust in Government – The Significance of Modernism, Political Cynicism and Integration". Paper to be presented on the EGPA Annual Conference, Oeiras 3-6 September 2003. Oeiras, Portugal: EGPA.

Cobb, J. and H. Daly. 1989. *For the Common Good: Redirecting the Economy toward Community, the Environment, and a Sustainable Future*. Boston: Beacon Press.

Cobb, C.W. and C. Rixfors. 1998. *Lessons Learned from the History of Social Indicators*. San Francisco: Redefining Progress.

Coelli, T., D.S. Prasada Rao and G. Battese. 1999. *An Introduction to Efficiency and Productivity Analysis*. Boston: Kluwer Academic Publishers.

Comptroller and Auditor General. 2001. *Measuring the Performance of Government Departments*. London: National Audit Office.

Cowell, R., J. Downe, S. Martin and A. Chen. 2006. "Making Sense of Service Improvement: An Empirical Analysis of Public Confidence in Local Government". Paper Presented to the 56th Political Studies Association Annual Conference, University of Reading, April 2006. Cardiff, United Kingdom: Centre for Local and Regional Government Research.

Cowper, J. and M. Samuels. 1997. "Performance Benchmarking in the Public Sector: The United Kingdom Experience". *Benchmarking, Evaluation and Strategic Management in the Public Sector*. Paris: OECD.

Crozier, M., S. Huntington and J. Watanuki. 1975. *The Crisis of Democracy*. New York: New York University Press.

Curristine, T. 2005. "Performance Information in the Budget Process: Results of OECD 2005 Questionnaire". *OECD Journal on Budgeting*. 5(2).

Davies, H.T.O., S.M. Nutley and P.C. Smith. 2000. *What Works? Evidence-Based Policy and Practice in Public Services*. Bristol: The Policy Press.

Dawson, D., H. Gravelle, M. O'Mahony, A. Street, M. Waele, A. Castelli, R. Jacobs, P. Kind, P. Loveridge, S. Martin, P. Stephens and L. Stokes. 2005. "Developing New Approaches to Measuring NHS Outputs and Productivity". York and London, United Kingdom: Centre for Health Economics at the University of York and the National Institute for Economic and Social Research.

Dervitsiotis, K. 1998. "The Challenge of Managing Organizational Change: Exploring the Relationship of Re-Engineering, Developing Learning Organizations and Total Quality Management". *Total Quality Management*. 9 (1).

Doig, A., S. McIvor and R. Theobald. 2006. "Numbers, Nuances and Moving Targets: Converging the Use of Corruption Indicators or Descriptors in Assessing State Development". *International Review of Administrative Sciences*. 72(2). 239-52.

Dooren, W van. 2005. "What Makes Organisations Measure? Hypotheses on the Causes and Conditions for Performance Measurement". *Financial Accountability and Management.* 21(3). 363-83.

Dooren, W van. 2006. "Performance Measurement in the Flemish Public Sector: A Supply and Demand Approach". PhD Thesis. Katholieke Universiteit. Leuven, Belgium.

Dooren, W. van and M. Aristigueta. 2005. "The Rediscovery of Social Indicators in Europe and the USA: An International Comparison". Paper presented at the EGPA annual conference 2005 (30 August – 9 September 2005). Bern, Switzerland.

Dooren, W. van and M. Sterck. 2006, "Financial Management Reforms after a Political Shift: A Transformative Perspective". *International Journal of Productivity and Performance Management.* 6 (55).

Dooren, W. van, M. Sterck and G. Bouckaert. 2006. "Recent Developments in Output Measurement within the Public Sector". Unpublished report prepared for the Organisation for Economic Co-operation and Development. Paris: OECD.

Dubnik, M. J. 1998. "Clarifying Accountability: An Ethical Theory Framework". In C. Sampford, N. Preston and C.-A. Bois (eds.) *Public Sector Ethics: Finding and Implementing Values.* London: Routledge.

Dunn, D. 1997. *Politics and Administration at the Top - Lessons from Down Under.* Pittsburgh: University of Pittsburgh Press.

East, P. 1997. "From Outputs to Outcomes: Opening Address to the Public Service Senior Management Conference". Wellington, New Zealand. 9 October 1997.

Economic and Social Research Council. 2005. "Where Does Britain Rank? - International Public Services Rankings". Report on a conference held 13 December 2005. London, UK. *www.publicservices.ac.uk/wp-content/uploads/rankingsconferencereport.pdf*

European Commission. 2006. Public Opinion Analysis Web site. *http://ec.europa.eu/public_opinion/index_en.htm.* Accessed 10 September 2006.

European Institution of Public Administration. 2002. *Common Assessment Framework (CAF): Improving an Organisation through Self Assessment 2002.* Maastricht: European Institute of Public Administration.

European Sourcebook of Crime and Criminal Justice Statistics. 2003. Den Haag: Wetenschappelijk Onderzoek- en Documentatiecentrum.

Eurostat. 2001. *Handbook on Price and Volume Measures in National Accounts*. Luxembourg: Office for Official Publications of the European Communities.

Eurostat. 2005. *Measuring Progress Towards a More Sustainable Europe*. Luxembourg: Office for Official Publications of the European Communities.

Fischer, T., O. Heilwagen, L. Novy, M. Brusis and J. Ramel. 2006. "Concept for a New Index of Reform Capacity". Gütersloh and Munich: Bertelsmann Foundation and the Centre for Applied Policy Research.

Gallais, A. 2006. "Proposal of an Output Method for PPP on (Non-Market) Education". Paris: OECD (Statistics Directorate).

Garrett, R., J. Thurber, A. Fritschler and D. Rosenbloom. 2006. "Assessing the Impact of Bureaucracy Bashing by Electoral Campaigns". *Public Administration Review*. 66(2). 228-40.

Giovannini, E. and A. Uyshal. 2006. *Statistics, Knowledge and Policy: What do We Know about What People Know*. Paris: OECD. Presented to the OECD Workshop on Business and Consumer Tendency Surveys, Rome September 2006.

Goetz, K. 2001. "Executive Governance in Central and Eastern Europe (Special Issue)". *Journal of European Public Policy*. 8(6).

Goodhart, C.A.E. 1975. "Problems of Monetary Management: The UK Experience". *Papers in Monetary Economics*. I. Reserve Bank of Australia.

Gormley, W.T. and D. L. Weimer. 1999. *Organizational Report Cards*. Cambridge, Mass.: Harvard University Press.

Gregory, R. 1995. "Accountability, Responsibility and Corruption: Managing the 'Public Production Process'" in J. Boston (ed.) *The State under Contract*. Wellington: Bridget Williams Books Ltd.

Gregory, R. 2004. "Political Life and Intervention Logic: Relearning Old Lessons?" *International Public Management Review*. 5(2). 1-12.

Grizzle, G. 2002. "Performance Measurement and Dysfunction: The Dark Side of Quantifying Work". *Public Performance and Management Review*. 25 (4). 363-9.

H.M. Treasury. 2001. "2000 Spending Review, Chapter 9: Foreign and Commonwealth Office". White paper. H.M. Treasury. London, UK. *www.hm-treasury.gov.uk/pss_psa_fco.htm*.

Hackman, J. and G. Oldman. 1980. *Work Redesign*. Reading, Mass.: Addison-Wesley.

Hagen, J von. 1992. *Budgeting Procedures and Fiscal Performance in the European Communities*. Brussels: Directorate General for Economic and Financial Affairs, Commission of the European Communities.

Hagen, J von and I. Harden. 1995. "Budget Processes and Commitment to Fiscal Discipline". *European Economic Review*. 39(3-4). 771-9.

Hall, J., C. Carswell, R. Jones and D. Yencken. 2005. "Collaborating with Civil Society: Reflections from Australia" in *Statistics, Knowledge and Policy: Key Indicators to Inform Decision Making*. Paris: OECD. 434-452.

Hallerberg, M. 2004. *Domestic Budgets in a United Europe*. Ithaca: Cornell University Press.

Hallerberg, M. and J. von Hagen. 1997. *Electoral Institutions, Cabinet Negotiations, and Budget Deficits in the European Union (NBER Working Paper 6341)*. Cambridge, Mass.: National Bureau of Economic Research.

Hallerberg, M., R. Strauch and J. von Hagen. 2001. "The Use and Effectiveness of Budgetary Rules and Norms in EU Member States". Report Prepared for the Dutch Ministry of Finance. Bonn, Germany: Institute of European Integration Studies.

Hann, J. de, W. Moesen and B. Volkerink. 1999. "Budgetary Procedures – Aspects and Changes: New Evidence for Some European Countries" in J. M. Poterba and J. v. Hagen (eds.) *Fiscal Institutions and Fiscal Performance*. Chicago: University of Chicago Press. 265-300.

Hatry, H.P. 1999. *Performance Measurement: Getting Results*. Washington, D.C.: Urban Institute Press.

Hatry, H.P. 2004. *Public and Private Agencies Need to Manage for Results, Not Just Measure Them*. Washington, D.C.: Urban Institute Press.

Hatry, H.P., E. Morley, S. Rossman and J. Wholey. 2003. *How Federal Programs Use Outcome Information: Opportunities for Federal Managers*. Washington, D.C.: IBM Endowment for the Business of Government and the National Academy of Public Administration.

Heinrich, C.J. 1999. "Do Government Bureaucrats Make Effective Use of Performance Management Information?" *Journal of Public Administration Research and Theory*. 9 (3). 363-93.

Heintzman, R. and B. Marson. 2005. "People, Service and Trust: Is There a Public Sector Service Value Chain?" (*http://ras.sagepub.com/cgi/content/short/71/4/549*). *International Review of Administrative Sciences*. 71(4). 549-75.

Hood, C. 1974. "Administrative Diseases". *Public Administration* (52).

Hood, C. 2005. "Public Management: The Word, the Movement, the Science" in E. Ferlie, L. Lynn Jr. and C. Pollitt (eds.) *The Oxford Handbook of Public Management*. Oxford: Oxford University Press. 7-26.

Hood, C., M. Lodge and C. Clifford. 2002. "Civil Service Policy-Making Competencies in the German BMWi and the British DTI". *Industry Forum*. London.

Hood, C. and B.G. Peters. 2004. "The Middle-Ageing of New Public Management: Into the Age of Paradox?" *Journal of Public Administration Research and Theory*. 14 (3). 267-82.

Humphreys, P. 2003. "Quality, Satisfaction and Trust from the Perspective of Irish Public Service Modernisation". Paper to be presented on the EGPA Annual Conference, Oeiras 3-6 September 2003. Oeiras, Portugal: EGPA.

International Monetary Fund and World Bank. 2006. *Global Monitoring Report 2006: Strengthening Mutual Accountability – Aid, Trade and Governance*. Washington, D.C.: Development Committee of the International Monetary Fund and the World Bank.

James, O. 2000. "Regulation Inside Government: Public Interest Justifications and Regulatory Failures". *Public Administration*. 78 (2). 327-43.

James, O. 2004. "The UK Core Executive's Use of Public Service Agreements as a Tool of Governance". *Public Administration*. 82(2). 397-419.

Joumard, I., P. Kongsrud, Y. Nam and R. Price. 2004. "Enhancing the Cost Effectiveness of Public Spending: Experience in OECD Countries". *OECD Economic Studies*. 2003/2 (37). 109-61.

Kampen, J., S. Van de Walle and G. Bouckaert. 2003. "On the Relative Role of the Public Administration, the Public Services and the Political Institutions in Building Trust in Government in Flanders". Paper Prepared for the ASPA 64th National Conference 'the Power of Public Service', Washington, D.C., 15-18 March 2003. Leuven: Public Management Institute, Katholieke Universiteit.

Kaufman, H. 1956. "Emerging Conflicts in the Doctrines of Public Administration". *American Political Science Review*. 50 (4). 1057-1073.

Kaufmann, D., A. Kraay and P. Zoido-Lobaton. 1999. "Aggregating Governance Indicators (World Bank Policy Research Working Paper No. 2195)". Washington, D.C.: World Bank.

Kettl, D. F. 2000. *The Global Public Management Revolution: A Report on the Transformation of Governance*. Washington, D.C.: Brookings Institution Press.

Killerby, P. 2005. "'Trust Me, I'm from the Government': The Complex Relationship between Trust in Government and Quality of Governance". *Social Policy Journal of New Zealand* (25).

Knack, S. 2006. "Measuring Corruption in Eastern Europe and Central Asia: a Critique of the Cross-Country Indicators". World Bank Policy Research Department Working Paper 3968. World Bank, Washington, D.C.

Knack, S., M. Kugler and N. Manning. 2003. "Second Generation Governance Indicators". *International Review of Administrative Sciences*. 69(3). 345-64.

Knack, S. and N. Manning. 2000. "Towards Consensus on Governance Indicators: Selecting Public Management and Broader Governance Indicators". Paper presented at the joint UN/OECD/World Bank/IMF International Development Forum, March 2000. Washington, D.C.

Kraan, D. and J. Kelly. 2005. *Reallocation: The Role of Budgetary Institutions*. Paris: OECD.

Kristensen, J.K., W.S. Groszyk and B. Bühler. 2001. "Outcome-Focused Management and Budgeting". *OECD Journal on Budgeting*. 1(4). Paris: OECD. 7-34.

Kuhry, B., V. Veldheer and J. Stevens. 2005. *Maten Voor Gemeenten*. Den Haag: Social and Cultural Planning Office.

Lequiller, F. 2005. "Measurement of Non-Market Volume Output". Clarification Item C10 for Fourth Meeting of the Advisory Expert Group on National Accounts, 30 January - 8 February 2006, Frankfurt. Paris: OECD.

Light, P. 2006. "The Tides of Reform Revisited: Patterns in Making Government Work, 1945-2002". *Public Administration Review*. 66 (1). 6-19.

Lonti, Z. and R. Gregory. 2006. "Accountability or Countability Performance Measurement in the New Zealand Public Service, 1992-2002". *Australian Journal of Public Administration.*

Manning, N. and N. Parison. 2003. "International Public Administration Reform : Implications for the Russian Federation". *Directions in Development.* Washington, D.C.: World Bank.

Marmor, T., R. Freeman and K. Okma. 2005. "Comparative Perspectives and Policy Learning in the World of Health Care". *Journal of Comparative Policy Analysis.* 7 (4). 331-48.

Matheson, A., B. Weber, N. Manning and E. Arnould. 2007. "Study on the Political Involvement in Senior Staffing and on the Delineation of Responsibilities Between Ministers and Senior Civil Servants". *OECD Working Papers on Public Governance.* 2007/6. Paris: OECD.

Matthews, E. 2006. "Measuring Well-Being and Societal Progress: A Brief History and the Latest News". Prepared for the Joint OECD-JRC Workshop "Measuring Well-Being and Societal Progress", 19-21 June 2006, Milan. Paris: OECD.

Mayne, J. 1999. "Addressing Attribution through Contribution Analysis: Using Performance Measures Sensibly". Working paper. Office of the Auditor General of Canada. Ottawa, Canada. *www.oag-bvg.gc.ca/internet/docs/99dp1_e.pdf.*

Michalos, A.C. 2006. "Political Culture and Well-Being: Beyond Government Services". First Draft for Discussion at the JRC/OECD Workshop on Measuring Well-Being and Societal Progress - Milan, 19-21 June 2006. Paris: OECD.

Moore, M. 1995. *Creating Public Value: Strategic Management in Government.* Cambridge, Mass., Harvard University Press.

Mosher, F. 1968. *Democracy and the Public Service.* New York: Oxford University Press.

Munoz, P. 2005. "Indicators for EU Policy Making: The Example of Structural Indicators" in *Statistics, Knowledge and Policy: Key Indicators to Inform Decision Making.* Paris: OECD. 385-98.

Musgrave, R. and P. Musgrave. 1984. *Public Finance in Theory and Practice* (Fourth Edition). San Francisco: McGraw Hill.

Nardo, M., M. Saisana, A. Saltelli, S. Tarantola, A. Hoffman and E. Giovanni. 2005. *OECD Handbook on Constructing Composite Indicators: Methodology and User Guide.* Paris: OECD.

National Audit Office. 2005. *Public Service Agreements: Managing Data Quality - Compendium Report.* London: National Audit Office.

Nevitte, N. 2006. *The Decline of Deference: Canadian Value Change in Cross National Perspective.* Broadview Press.

New Zealand State Services Commission. 2003. "Guidance on Outcomes Focused Management – Building Block 3: Intervention Logic (Version 2.1)." Wellington: State Services Commission. *http://io.ssc.govt.nz/pathfinder/documents/pathfinder-BB3-intervention_logic.pdf.*

New Zealand State Services Commission. 2006. *State of the Development Goals Report 2006.* Wellington: State Services Commission.

Noll, H. 1996. *Social Indicators and Social Reporting: The International Experience.* Ottawa: Social Indicators Symposium, 4-5 October 1996, Canadian Council on Social Development.

Nove, A. 1958. "The Problem of Success Indicators in Soviet Industry". *Economica* (New Series). 25 (97). 1-13.

Nye, S., P.D. Zelikow and D.C. King. 1997. *Why People Don't Trust Government.* Cambridge, Massachusetts: Harvard University Press.

O'Mahony, M. and P.A. Stevens. 2004. "International Comparisons of Performance in the Provision of Public Services: Outcome Based Measures for Education". Paper Presented to the Royal Economic Society Annual Conference, Swansea.

OECD. 1982. "The OECD List of Social Indicators". *Social Indicator Development Programme, no. 5.* Paris: OECD.

OECD. 2000. *Trust in Government: Ethics Measures in OECD Countries.* Paris: OECD.

OECD. 2001a. *Citizens as Partners: Information, Consultation and Participation in Policy-Making.* Paris: OECD.

OECD. 2001b. *Measuring Productivity OECD Manual: Measurement of Aggregate and Industry-Level Productivity Growth.* Paris: OECD.

OECD. 2001c. *The Wellbeing of Nations: The Role of Human and Social Capital, Education and Skills.* Paris: OECD.

OECD. 2002. "Overview of Results-Focused Management and Budgeting in OECD Member Countries". PUMA/SBO(2002)1. Paris: OECD. *http://www.olis.oecd.org/olis/2002doc.nsf/LinkTo/PUMA-SBO(2002)1*

OECD. 2003a. *Managing Conflict of Interest in the Public Service. OECD Guidelines and Country Experiences.* Paris: OECD.

OECD. 2003b. *Quality Framework and Guidelines for OECD Statistical Activities (Version 2003/1).* Paris: OECD.

OECD. 2004. *Glossary of Statistical Terms 2004. (http://stats.oecd.org/glossary/glossary.pdf).* Paris: OECD.

OECD. 2005a. *Managing Conflict of Interest in the Public Sector: A Toolkit.* Paris: OECD.

OECD. 2005b. "Management in Government: Feasibility Report on the Development of Comparative Data (Technical Annexes)". GOV/PGC(2005)10/ANN. Paris: OECD. *www.olis.oecd.org/olis/2005doc.nsf/LinkTo/NT00004492/$FILE/JT0019 4378.PDF*

OECD. 2005c. *Modernising Government: The Way Forward.* Paris: OECD.

OECD. 2005d. *Society at a Glance: OECD Social Indicators 2005 Edition.* Paris: OECD.

OECD. 2005e. "Solving the Pensions Puzzle". OECD Policy Brief. Paris: OECD. *http://www.oecd.org/dataoecd/53/19/34587956.pdf*

OECD. 2006. *Cutting Red Tape: National Strategies for Administrative Simplification.* Paris: OECD.

OECD. 2007. "Towards Better Measurement of Government". *OECD Working Papers on Public Governance* 2007/1. Paris: OECD.

OECD. 2008. *Employment in the Government in the Perspective of the Production Costs of Goods and Services in the Public Domain.* OECD/GOV/PGC/PEM(2008)1. Paris: OECD.

Perrin, B. 1998. "Effective Use and Misuse of Performance Measurement". *American Journal of Evaluation.* 19 (3). 367-79.

Perrin, B. 2006. "Moving from Outputs to Outcomes: Practical Advice from Governments around the World". *Managing for Performance and Results Series.* Washington, D.C.: IBM Center for the Business of Government and the World Bank.

Perry, P. and A. Webster. 1999. *New Zealand Politics at the Turn of the Millennium: Attitudes and Values about Politics and Government.* Auckland, New Zealand: Alpha Publications.

Plantz, M., M. Taylor Greenway and M. Hendricks. 1997. *Outcome Measurement: Showing Results in the Non-profit Sector.* United Way of America.

Polackova, H. 1999. "Contingent Liabilities – A Threat to Fiscal Stability". PREM Note Economic Policy No. 9. Washington, D.C.: World Bank. *http://www1.worldbank.org/prem/PREMNotes/premnote9.pdf.*

Pollitt, C. 1995. "Justification by Works or by Faith". *Evaluation.* 1(2). 133-54.

Pollitt, C. 1997. "Looking Outcomes in the Face: The Limits of Government Action". Address to the Public Service Senior Management Conference, Wellington, New Zealand, 9 October 1997.

Pollitt, C. 2001. "Integrating Financial Management and Performance Management". *OECD Journal on Budgeting.* 1(2). 7-38.

Pollitt, C. 2006. "Performance Information for Democracy: The Missing Link?" *Evaluation.* 12:1. 38-55.

Pollitt, C. and G. Bouckaert. 2003. "Evaluating Public Management Reforms: An International Perspective". In H. Wollman (ed.) *Evaluation in Public Sector Reform.* Cheltenham, United Kingdom: Edward Elgar. 12-35.

Pollitt, C. and G. Bouckaert. 2004. *Public Management Reform: A Comparative Analysis.* Oxford, United Kingdom: Oxford University Press.

Pollitt, C.; C. Talbot, J. Caulfield and A. Smullen. 2004. *Agencies: How Governments do Things through Semi-autonomous Organizations,* Basingstoke: Palgrave/Macmillan.

Porta, R. La, F. Lopez-de-Silane, A. Shleifer and R. Vishny. 1998. "The Quality of Government". *Journal of Law Economics and Organization.* 15 (April). 222-79.

Poterba, J. and J. von Hagen. 1999. "Fiscal Institutions and Fiscal Performance". Conference Report, National Bureau of Economic Research. Chicago: University of Chicago Press.

Pritchard, A. 2003. "Understanding Government Output and Productivity". *Economic Trends* (596).

Propper, C. and D. Wilson. 2003. *The Use and Usefulness of Performance Measures in the Public Sector (CMPO Working Paper Series No. 03/073).* Bristol, United Kingdom: The Centre for Market And Public Organisation.

Public Administration Select Committee. 2003. "On Target? Government by Measurement". Fifth Report of Session 2002–03, Volume I. London: House of Commons. *www.publications.parliament.uk/pa/cm200203/cmselect/cmpubadm/62/6 2.pdf.*

Public Sector Accounting Board. 2006. *CICA Public Sector Accounting Handbook* (as updated at October 2006). Toronto: Canadian Institute of Chartered Accountants.

Raaum, R. and S. Morgan. 2001. *Performance Auditing: A Measurement Approach.* Altamonte Springs: The Institute of Internal Auditors.

Radin, B. 2006. *Challenging the Performance Movement: Accountability, Complexity and Democratic Values.* Washington, D.C.: Georgetown University Press.

Riche, M. 2003. *Developing Key National Indicators.* Washington, D.C.: Government Accountability Office.

Rosenthal, A. 1997. *The Decline of Representative Democracy: Process, Participation, and Power in State Legislatures.* Washington, D.C.: Congressional Quarterly Books.

Ryzin, G van., D. Muzzio, S. Immerwahr, L. Gulick and E. Martinez. 2004. "Drivers and Consequences of Citizen Satisfaction: An Application of the American Customer Satisfaction Index Model to New York City". *Public Administration Review.* 64(3). 331-41.

Samuelson, P. 1954. "The Pure Theory of Public Expenditure". *Review of Economics and Statistics.* 36 (4). 387-9.

Savage, J. 2005. "Political Development and Fiscal Outcomes (Paper Prepared for the "Long-Term Budget Challenge: Public Finance and Fiscal Sustainability in the G-7". Conference, Washington, D.C., 2-4 June 2005. Charlottesville, Virginia: University of Virginia.

Scheirer, M.A. 1994. "Designing and Using Process Evaluation" in J. S. Wholey, H. P. Hatry and K. E. Newcomer (eds.) *Handbook of Practical Program Evaluation.* San Francisco: Jossey-Bass. 40-68.

Schick, A. 1996. "Why Most Developing Countries Should Not Try the New Zealand Reforms". *World Bank Observer.* 13. 123.

Schick, A. 2003. "The Role of Fiscal Rules in Budgeting". *OECD Journal on Budgeting.* 3(3). 7-34.

Schick, A. 2005. "The Performing State: Reflection on an Idea Whose Time Has Come But Whose Implementation Has Not". *OECD Journal on Budgeting*. 3(2). Paris: OECD.

Scott, G. 2001. *Public Management in New Zealand: Lessons and Challenges*. Wellington: New Zealand Business Roundtable.

Self, P. 1972. *Administrative Theories and Politics - an Inquiry into the Structure and Processes of Modern Government*. London: Allen and Unwin.

Sharman, L. 2001. *Holding to Account: The Review of Audit and Accountability for Central Government*. London: H.M Treasury.

Smith, P. 1995. "On the Unintended Consequences of Publishing Performance Data in the Public Sector". *International Journal of Public Administration*. 18. 277-310.

Social and Cultural Planning Office. 2004. *Public Sector Performance: An International Comparison of Education, Health Care, Law and Order, and Public Administration*. The Hague: Social and Cultural Planning Office.

Sterck, M., W. Van Dooren and G. Bouckaert. 2006. "Performance Measurement for Sub-National Service Delivery". Unpublished report prepared for the Organisation of Economic Co-operation and Development. Paris: OECD.

Sudders, M. and J. Nahem. 2004. *Governance Indicators: A Users' Guide*. Oslo: UNDP.

Suleiman, E. 2005. *Dismantling Democratic States*. Princeton, New Jersey: Princeton University Press.

Summers, R. and A. Heston. 1999. "The World Distribution of Well-Being Dissected" in A. Heston and R. E. Lipsey (eds.) *International and Interarea Comparisons of Income, Output, and Prices*. 479-503.

Sutherland, D., R. Price and I. Joumard. 2005. *Fiscal Rules for Sub-Central Governments: Design and Impact (Economics Department Working Paper No. 465)*. Paris: OECD.

Talbot, C. 1996. *Ministers and Agencies: Control, Performance and Accountability*. London: CIPFA.

Talbot, C. 2003. "Reinventing Government: Performance, Evaluation and Outcomes". *NIRA Policy Research*. 16(5).

Talbot, C. and C. Johnson. 2006. "Seasonal Cycles in Public Management: Disaggregation and Re-Aggregation". *Public Money and Management*.